OSPREY AIRCRAFT OF THE ACES® • 78

SE 5/5a
Aces of World War 1

SERIES EDITOR: TONY HOLMES

OSPREY AIRCRAFT OF THE ACES® • 78

SE 5/5a
Aces of World War 1

Norman Franks

OSPREY
PUBLISHING

FRONT COVER

Flying with No 2 Sqn, Australian Flying Corps (AFC), Victorian Lt George J Cox was one of 13 pilots to 'make ace' with the unit. Born in the Melbourne suburb of Carlton on 17 July 1894, he joined the unit in early 1918. Cox claimed his first kill on 30 May and achieved his fifth on the morning of 27 August when his flight tangled with a large formation of Fokker D VII and Pfalz D III scouts over Sains-les-Marquion, west of Cambrai. He was flying SE 5a E5965 at the time, and his combat report for the mission read as follows;

'Whilst on patrol with my flight, 30 Fokker biplanes were encountered over Sains at a height of 17,000 ft at 1050 hrs. I dived on the rear machine and fired a short burst of 50 rounds at it. I noticed that it immediately emitted smoke from behind the pilot's seat and flames from the tail, before shortly afterwards bursting into a mass of flames. I then zoomed up and dived on another machine from behind, firing a good, long burst from 150 yards. The enemy aircraft zoomed up and seemed to fall over on its side, then did a straight nose dive, which I followed for about 6000 ft until it was impossible to see him any further.

'I then climbed southeast and encountered a Pfalz scout at about 17,000 ft. I dived on him, putting in a long burst from 150 to 50 yards range. He turned over and went down, out of control, in a slow spiral, which I watched for about 3000 ft until the presence of five Fokker biplanes, which were firing at me, diverted my attention.'

Fellow aces Capt Roby Manuel and Lt Frank Alberry both confirmed seeing the Fokker D VII going down in flames, and Cox's combat report was countersigned by the leader of No 80 Wing, Lt Col Louis A Strange DSO MC DFC. With these three victories, George Cox became an ace. However, he had not scored again by the time he was shot down behind enemy lines in E5965 on 21 September and made a Prisoner of War – his SE 5a had been struck by a stray artillery shell over Armentières (*Cover artwork by Mark Postlethwaite*)

First published in Great Britain in 2007 by Osprey Publishing
Midland House, West Way, Botley, Oxford, OX2 0PH, UK
443 Park Avenue South, New York, NY, 10016, USA
E-mail: info@ospreypublishing.com

ISBN 978 1 84603 180 9

Edited by Tony Holmes
Page design by Tony Truscott
Typeset in Adobe Garamond and Univers
Cover Artwork by Mark Postlethwaite
Aircraft Profiles by Harry Dempsey
Index by Alan Thatcher
Originated by PDQ Digital Media Solutions
Printed and bound in China through Bookbuilders

07 08 09 10 11   10 9 8 7 6 5 4 3 2 1

For a catalogue of all books published by Osprey please contact:
NORTH AMERICA
Osprey Direct, c/o Random House Distribution Center, 400 Hahn Road, Westminster, MD, 21157
E-mail: info@ospreydirect.com
ALL OTHER REGIONS
Osprey Direct UK, PO Box 140 Wellingborough, Northants, NN8 2FA, UK
E-mail: info@ospreydirect.co.uk
www.ospreypublishing.com

ACKNOWLEDGEMENTS

I am continually grateful to friends and fellow authors for their generous help, especially by way of photographs. Tony Mellor-Ellis continues to be an amazing source for images of World War 1 airmen and aeroplanes, and I am in awe of E Frank Cheesman's collection, especially of faces – he is able to find photographs of many airmen from the Great War that have for many years been merely names to me. My thanks also goes to friends Mike O'Connor, Andy Thomas and Les Rogers, as well as Stuart Leslie, who, until recently, shared a massive archive with the late Jack Bruce – Stuart has always been more than willing to share things with others.

Readers will find several references to SE 5/5a pilots from World War 1 that I had the good fortune to either know or correspond with, sadly all now departed, but I still thank them for their youthful courage and their later kindness in relating their recollections of the Great War.

CONTENTS

A NEW BREED OF FIGHTER

When interest in World War 1 aviation enjoyed a revival in the 1950s, aviation historians at the time quickly began to compare the SE 5/5a and the Sopwith Camel of the Great War with the Spitfire and Hurricane of World War 2. I suppose, to a small degree, there is some sense to this, but they were both totally unique fighters in their own right.

As we saw in *Osprey Aircraft of the Aces 52 – Sopwith Camel Aces of World War 1*, the pugnacious Camel had an unmatched rate of turn thanks to its forward centre of gravity (engine, pilot, guns and petrol tank all up front). This manoeuvrability, when combined with its twin Vickers machine guns firing through the propeller, made the Sopwith fighter a formidable opponent in the air. It was also superior to the SE 5 as a ground attack platform thanks to the pilot's seating position further forward in the Camel. This meant that he had better visibility of the target he was strafing and bombing.

With the Camel revelling in medium to low altitude combat, the SE 5/5a was left to hold its own at higher ceilings. Fortunately for the Royal Flying Corps (RFC) and Royal Air Force (RAF), the SE 5/5a was the superior aircraft at altitudes exceeding 10,000 ft in any case. Therefore, squadrons equipped with the fighter tended to be used more for aerial combat at medium to high altitudes, and much less in the air-to-ground role. Furthermore, the SE 5/5a's armament of one forward-firing Vickers machine gun in front of the pilot and a single Lewis gun affixed to the top wing – identical to the armament fitted to the Nieuport Scouts that preceded them – made the aircraft ideal for stalking high-flying prey. Pilots could sneak up beneath a hostile machine, ratchet down the gun and fire up into the underbelly of the enemy aircraft.

Not everyone was keen on the SE 5/5a's armament, however, with eight-victory ace Capt Cecil Lewis MC (Military Cross) of No 56 Sqn stating that he thought it 'strange'. He – and others – wondered why the new fighter did not have twin fixed Vickers guns, instead of just one, with the Lewis on the top wing deleted altogether. While the latter did carry a double capacity drum containing 100 rounds, this needed to be replaced when empty with extra drums kept by the pilot's seat.

Pulling down the gun was not difficult, helped by the slipstream, but removing the empty drum in

These two 7.7 mm (0.303 in) weapons were the most important aircraft guns used by the Allies in World War 1. Seen in its ground-based form in the upper photograph, the Lewis gun was a gas-operated weapon supplied with ammunition from a 47-round single-row or 97-round twin-row drum magazine, and in its aerial form was modified with a spade grip rather than a stocked butt. It also had the barrel and gas cylinder radiator either removed or replaced by a light aluminium casing in an effort to save weight. The Vickers gun was revised with air rather than water cooling (typified by a louvered air-cooling casing in place of the ground-based weapon's water-cooling jacket), and was supplied with ammunition from a belt drawn from a magazine in the fuselage *(Bruce Robertson)*

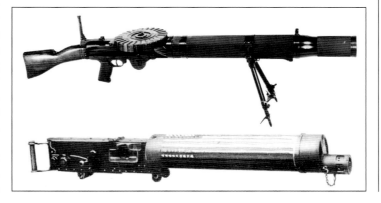

the same slipstream could smack it into the pilot's face, and getting the gun back up was no easy task either. Cecil Lewis thought it a typical factory invention which could never have been devised by a pilot who had combat experience. One wonders, nevertheless, whether future 44-victory ace Capt Albert Ball VC (Victoria Cross) DSO (Distinguished Service Order) and two Bars MC, also of No 56 Sqn, had anything to do with it, having become used to such an installation in his Nieuport Scouts in 1916–17. Indeed, Ball had test flown the SE 5 prototype during a rest from France.

This photograph illustrates how the pilot could move the top-wing Lewis gun along its mounting rail on the SE 5/5a. The weapon could be used to fire upwards from this position, and it usually had to be pulled down by the pilot in order for him to be able to change ammunition drums in flight

FIRST SQUADRON

Of the 14 SE 5/5a squadrons that served on the Western Front, four had converted from the Nieuport. However, the first unit to receive the new type was itself entirely new. No 56 Sqn had been formed around a nucleus supplied by No 28 Sqn in June 1916. Initially based at Gosport, in Hampshire, the unit had flown a mixed fleet of aircraft until issued with new SE 5s at London Colney, in Hertfordshire, in March 1917.

The Scout Experimental 5 was designed and built by the Royal Aircraft Factory at Farnborough, in Hampshire. The aircraft was created around the new, geared, Hispano-Suiza 8A engine, which had been designed by Marc Birkigt in the company's Barcelona factory in early 1915. The French adopted the engine for their aircraft very early on, and the British eventually followed suit in August 1915 when 50 were ordered. A licence was also granted to Wolseley at the same time so production of Hispano-Suiza engines could be undertaken in the UK. These were initially

With co-designer Maj Frank Goodden sat in the cockpit, this aircraft was the first of three SE 5 prototypes built by the Royal Aircraft Factory in mid-1916. The SE 5 soon matured into the SE 5a, with a more powerful engine and other minor airframe changes. It was, along with the Sopwith Camel, the finest British fighter of World War 1 *(Bruce Robertson)*

destined for the obsolescent BE 2c, but when the French fitted the engine into the all new SPAD fighting scout in 1916, it soon became apparent to the British that a new aircraft design was needed to accommodate the engine.

The Royal Aircraft Factory quickly came up with the working design of the SE 5 in June 1916, and the first prototype machines were tested that autumn with a 150 hp direct-drive Hispano-Suiza 8A engine. The prototype made its

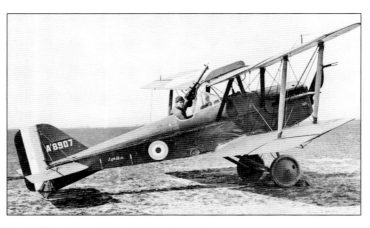

Seen here with Capt Albert Ball in the cockpit and the Lewis gun carried on the upper-wing centre section pulled back to fire obliquely forward and upward in the fashion much favoured by Ball, this SE 5 (A8907) has the original type of semi-cockpit transparency that was disliked by virtually all pilots and soon removed in favour of a small windscreen *(MARS)*

first flight on 22 November, with Maj Frank Goodden, who had helped in the initial design, at the controls. The following day, experienced ace Capt Albert Ball performed the aircraft's second flight whilst home on leave from France. His reaction was not favourable, however, for he stated that he much preferred the Nieuport 17 that he had enjoyed notable success with over previous months. Nevertheless, the SE 5 went into production, and No 56 Sqn began to receive them four months later.

One outstanding feature of the new fighter was a large 'glasshouse', which encircled half of the forward cockpit area. It was not liked by service pilots, however, who thought it cumbersome and a danger to the man in the cockpit in the event of a crash. Although authority was loath to have it removed, No 56 Sqn CO Maj R G Blomfield DSO discarded the 'glasshouse' in favour of a more standard windshield once his unit got to France.

An SE 5 had first gone to France during the Christmas 1916 period for frontline pilot evaluation, where the machine was generally accepted. After a few modifications, and installation of a 180 hp version of the 8A engine, the SE 5 entered production in Farnborough in early 1917. The first 24 aircraft to leave the Royal Aircraft Factory were sent to No 56 Sqn.

In anticipation of the new fighting scout arriving at London Colney, Maj Blomfield had been given something of a free hand in selecting his pilots. This was probably why the unit lived with the mystique of being a 'crack' squadron of aces once in action in France. Indeed, by late 1917 No 56 Sqn certainly had more than its share of aces, but this was not solely due to Blomfield's earlier selection.

As luck would have it, one of the unit's flight commanders was Capt Albert Ball, who, despite his misgivings, flew the SE 5. Such was his fame, however, he was allowed to have his own personal Nieuport 17 to use on lone sorties, while flying the SE 5 for flight patrol work.

And, ironically, it was this sole Nieuport that claimed No 56 Sqn's first victory over a German aircraft. Ball, with orders not to cross the trench lines, had led the first patrol on the morning of 22 April from the unit's base at Vert Galand. Spotting an Albatros two-seater close to the frontline, Ball attacked. What happened next could not have improved his feelings towards the SE 5, for despite firing three drums of Lewis gun ammunition, he observed no damage as the enemy aircraft headed back over German-held territory, where Ball had to break off his attack.

The following day, having discarded his SE 5, Ball went out alone in his Nieuport 17. Very few RFC pilots were still being allowed to patrol on their own by this stage of the war because German fighting scouts effectively ruled the skies over the Western Front. Only the more experienced aces could hope to survive, and Ball was one of them. Indeed, he had built his reputation in 1916 on boldly flying lone patrols deep into German territory.

Upon his return on 23 April, Ball could record one Albatros C-type destroyed. Later that morning he was out again, but this time in his SE 5 (A4850), and he claimed the aircraft's first victory when he flamed one of five Albatros scouts that he engaged. A short while later, during the same patrol, Ball forced another two-seater to land with a mortally wounded observer.

Albert Ball, perhaps the best known air ace on the Western Front during this period of the war, and still only 20 years of age, went on to claim a further eight or nine victories (all bar two with the SE 5) during his brief time with No 56 Sqn. As with his first success with the unit, Ball's last No 56 Sqn victory, claimed on 6 May, was scored in his Nieuport 17. The following day he was killed during a confused evening engagement with Albatros scouts from *Jagdstaffel* 11 in cloudy weather. The current consensus amongst aviation historians is that Ball became disorientated in thick cloud, and when he emerged in a dive, his SE 5 (A4850) was too low to pull out and it crashed near Annoeullin. In typically knightly fashion, the 44-victory ace died in the arms of a young French lady. A posthumous award of the Victoria Cross was announced in June 1917.

Despite this blow, not only to No 56 Sqn but to the RFC as a whole, which had lost its then leading ace, the unit carried on taking the war to the enemy. With C Flight's commander, Capt Henry Meintjes MC, also wounded in the 7 May fight that cost Ball his life, future 26-victory SE 5 ace Maj Gerald Maxwell temporarily took over Ball's flight until Capt Philip Prothero arrived. The latter, who would claim six of his eight victories in SE 5s, had previously served with No 24 Sqn – Prothero was on leave from the front when Ball was killed. Maj Geoffrey H Bowman (also a future SE 5 ace, with 22, of 32, victories claimed in the fighter) took over C Flight, while Capt C M Crowe (14, of 15, victories in the SE 5) continued to lead B Flight.

Having survived the tail end of 'Bloody April', which had seen German *Jastas* cutting swathes through RFC and Royal Naval Air Service units attempting to cover the British offensive at Arras, No 56 Sqn continued to engage the enemy into the summer. Although suffering periodic losses, the unit soon produced a handful of pilots who attained ace status.

Having developed a taste for success, these individuals continued to make claims even when the unit was pulled back to Bekesbourne, in Kent, in June 1917 to conduct Home Defence duties during the Gotha bomber

Before his death on 7 May 1917, Capt Albert Ball had been awarded the DSO and two Bars, MC and several foreign decorations, and had amassed 44 victories while serving with Nos 13, 11, 8, 60, 29 and 56 Sqns. He is seen here in the cockpit of a No 56 Sqn SE 5 soon after the unit had moved to France in April 1917. Ball was initially unimpressed by the new scout, preferring the agility of the Nieuport sesquiplane fighters he had enjoyed so much success with *(Bruce Robertson)*

Ball claimed nine of his 44 victories with the SE 5. One of the few British pilots to receive much press coverage during his life, Ball was essentially a lone flier who preferred to stalk his quarry through cloud cover rather than become involved in multi-aircraft dogfights *(Bruce Robertson)*

Maj G H 'Beery' Bowman claimed 22 victories with No 56 Sqn in 1917-18. He downed eight more aircraft leading No 41 Sqn between February and October 1918

Two of these pilots claimed significant scores with No 56 Sqn, namely (left) Capts James T B McCudden (57 victories) and (right) G J C Maxwell (26 victories). The third pilot is Capt I H D Henderson (*Bruce Robertson*)

threat. Amongst the high scorers during this period was 24-year-old Maj G H 'Beery' Bowman MC and Bar DSO DFC (Distinguished Flying Cross), who had started his career with No 29 Sqn. Hailing from the Old Trafford area of Manchester, he claimed five victories in June and six in July. By year-end, Bowman had increased his tally to 22. He scored two more victories in early 1918, before assuming command of No 41 Sqn towards the end of January. Bowman's score eventually rose to 32.

Fellow ace Gerald Joseph Constable Maxwell (in later life G J Constable Maxwell) enjoyed even greater success with No 56 Sqn than Bowman, claiming 26 victories. Hailing from Inverness, 20-year-old Maxwell was a nephew of Lord Lovat, who had formed the Lovat Scouts in January 1900 to fight in the Boer War. Like Bowman, Maxwell enjoyed a series of successes during the summer of 1917 following on from his first victory in April. By late September his score stood at 20, and he had been awarded the MC. In 1918, following a break from the action, Maxwell added a further six victories to his tally in the early summer, and received the DFC. Finishing the war with 26 victories to his credit, Maxwell scored no fewer than 12 of these in SE 5 B502.

Another of No 56 Sqn's early SE 5 aces was Welshman Capt Richard A Maybery, who was roughly the same age as Maxwell. Proud of his prior service with the 21st Empress of India's Lancers, he had seen action – and been seriously wounded – with this unit in the North West Frontier province until injured in a riding accident. Bored during his rehabilitation, and unable to sit on a horse, Maybery became involved in observing for an RFC unit that was based nearby. Travelling to Egypt to be trained as a pilot, he returned to France and joined No 56 Sqn in June 1917. Claiming a victory on his very first patrol with the unit, Maybery scored his first six successes in A8934. He was subsequently awarded the MC and Bar.

Unlike Bowman and Maxwell, Maybery did not survive the war, however, for he was shot down near Masnieres moments after claiming his 20th victory on 19 December. Maybery's CO, Maj R D Balcombe-Brown DSO, wrote to the mother of the young ace soon after he was killed, explaining that 'Your son had just crashed down his 20th Hun in flames when his own machine was seen to be going down. It was very misty, and the fighting was severe, and in the mist another German machine came from behind and above and shot him down'.

Also killed at the controls of a No 56 Sqn SE 5 was Lt Arthur P F Rhys Davids. A Londoner from Forest Hill, he was just 19 when he joined the unit in late 1916. The old Etonian racked up a score of

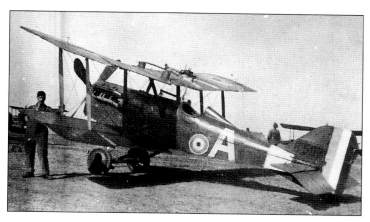

Capt G J C Maxwell used this SE 5 (B502) to claim 12 victories with No 56 Sqn between July and September 1917. Fellow ace Lt R A Maybery also downed two Albatros D IIIs with it on 10 August 1917 (*L A Rogers*)

Lt R A Maybery MC and Bar was another early SE 5 ace created by No 56 Sqn. He claimed six victories in July 1917 flying A8934, and had increased his tally to 21 by the time he was lost to flak on 20 December 1917. Maybery's final victory had come just 24 hours prior to his death in combat (*T Mellor-Ellis*)

Seen in the cockpit of his SE 5a, Lt A P F Rhys Davids of No 56 Sqn was credited with the 23 September 1917 shooting down of 48-victory ace Ltn Werner Voss. The latter was Rhys Davids' 19th victim (*Bruce Robertson*)

25 victories between May and October 1917, claiming three aircraft destroyed on 24 May and 5 September. In the famous fight with German ace Werner Voss on 23 September, in which the Fokker Dr I pilot scored hits on several SE 5s engaging him, it was Rhys Davids' fire that finally brought down the mercurial triplane pilot, who was three months younger than his victor.

Rhys Davids later wrote that he had wished he had brought Voss down alive, although in his actual combat it would seem that he spotted that the German was in trouble – his fuel pipe had almost certainly been damaged, for his engine was slowing. The British ace (flying SE 5a B525, in which he claimed his last eight victories) coolly lined up the German Fokker triplane and gave it the *coup de gras*. For his efforts Rhys Davids was awarded the DSO, MC and Bar. Sadly, on 27 October, he was killed in a fight with *Jasta* 2 Boelcke east of Roulers, becoming the fifth victim of ten-victory ace Ltn Karl Gallwitz.

Hailing from Toronto, Capt Reginald T C Hoidge was also an early member of No 56 Sqn. Having previously served with the Canadian Royal Garrison Artillery, Hoidge claimed his 16th and 17th victories on his 23rd birthday – 28 July 1917. By the end of October 1917 he had increased his score to 27 victories, and been awarded the MC and Bar. Rested shortly afterwards, he returned to the UK and served as an instructor for a year, before going back into action as a flight commander with No 1 Sqn in October 1918. Hoidge claimed one final success before Armistice Day, ending the war with 28 victories to his credit.

Another high-scoring ace with No 56 Sqn was Lt Leonard Monteagle Barlow of Islington, London, who achieved 20 victories between 24 April and 1 October 1917 – 15 of these were claimed either in SE 5as B507 or B511. He claimed double successes on 27 May and 17 August, and a triple on 25 September. The

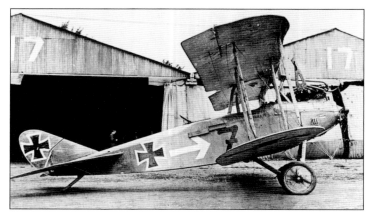

This DFW C V general-purpose biplane was brought down by Lt A P F Rhys Davids (in SE 5a A4563) north of Armentières on the afternoon of 12 July 1917 for his tenth victory (*Bruce Robertson*)

Lt L M Barlow MC and two Bars scored 20 victories with No 56 Sqn prior to being sent back to the UK to rest in September 1917. He was killed flight testing a Sopwith Dolphin in England in February 1918

The pioneer of dive and climb tactics for the SE 5, Maj C M Crowe MC DFC scored 14 victories with No 56 Sqn between April 1917 and July 1918 and a solitary success with No 85 Sqn in September 1918

recipient of the MC and two Bars, Barlow was sent back to the UK to rest in early October 1917, and was subsequently killed on 5 February 1918 when the Sopwith Dolphin that he was flight testing crashed at Martlesham Heath, in Suffolk.

A veteran of early action as an observer in 1915, 23-year-old Capt Cyril Marconi Crowe had subsequently learned to fly and been posted to another unit prior to joining No 56 Sqn as it received its first SE 5s in early 1917. Helping the less experienced pilots in the unit get to grips with the new fighting scout, Crowe soon revealed his abilities in combat by downing 15 German aircraft between April and July. Awarded the MC for his efforts, he then returned to the UK as an instructor, instilling in his pupils the 'dive and zoom' tactic that he and No 56 Sqn had done so much to perfect with the SE 5 during the spring and summer of 1917.

Crowe came back to France in August 1918 to take command of SE 5a-equipped No 85 Sqn, and he had gained one further victory, and the DFC, by war's end. In between these postings he had been given command of No 60 Sqn in July 1918, but as a result of a court martial following a fatal road accident, the ace had been demoted for a month, after which he was sent to No 85 Sqn.

No 56 Sqn produced still more aces during the summer of 1917, including Capt Eric Broadberry from Middlesex, who had previously served at Gallipoli with the Essex Regiment. He scored eight victories and received the MC in just a matter of weeks, but then suffered a serious leg wound during a fight with *Jasta* 6 on 11 July. He did not return to frontline duty. Squadronmate Lt Keith Muspratt also claimed eight victories and received an MC during this period. A doctor's son from Bournemouth, Muspratt was eventually sent back to the UK to rest, and he duly became a test pilot at Martlesham Heath. However, like 20-victory ace Lt L M Barlow, he was killed in a flying accident on 19 March 1918.

Twenty-year-old Lt Robert Sloley from Cape Town, South Africa, was another pilot to enjoy success in 1917, his nine victories being claimed between 14 August and 29 September. He was killed dog-fighting with 11-victory Xaver Dannhuber of *Jasta* 26 on 1 October.

No 56 Sqn's 'ace of aces' was James Thomas Byford McCudden, who also claimed his first successes with No 56 Sqn during the long summer of 1917. McCudden soon became the epitome of the new generation of war hero to emerge from this conflict. From humble beginnings to famed air ace, with every decoration his country could at that time bestow upon him, McCudden, more than anyone, typified the clean-cut, gallant youth – a mantle recently held by Albert Ball.

Born in Gillingham, Kent, on 28 March 1895, Jimmy McCudden was one of three sons who would all eventually be killed whilst serving as pilots in World War 1. His father was a quartermaster sergeant in the Army, and McCudden duly followed in his footsteps when he became a boy bugler with the Royal Engineers in 1910. Three years later he transferred to the RFC and became a mechanic, travelling to France with No 3 Sqn in August 1914. McCudden was occasionally allowed to fly as an aerial observer whilst serving with the unit, and in January 1916 he returned to Farnborough to learn to fly. Completing the course in April, he was transferred to FE 2-equipped No 20 Sqn at Clairmarais, near St-Omer, two months later.

In July, McCudden joined No 29 Sqn, which was flying the Airco DH 2 pusher scout. Two months later he made his first aerial claim, and his undoubted ability as a fighter pilot saw him progress from NCO to commissioned rank purely on his achievements in the air. Soon made a flight commander, and the leader of men, McCudden survived an action with Baron Manfred von Richthofen on 27 December 1916 which saw the latter claim him as his 15th victim! McCudden, who returned to base in his DH 2 without so much as a scratch, was unaware that his opponent during this patrol had been none other than von Richthofen.

By the time McCudden was sent back to the UK for a rest in February 1917, he had claimed five victories and received the Military Medal (MM), his first MC and the Belgian *Croix de Guerre* (CdG). He joined No 66 Sqn shortly afterwards, this unit having just re-equipped with Sopwith Pups. In June 1917, McCudden was posted to No 56 Sqn as a flight commander, the ace joining the unit with seven victories already to his credit. He immediately took to the new SE 5a, examples of which had begun to reach the unit just prior to McCudden's arrival.

The SE 5a featured the 200 hp geared Hispano-Suiza 8B in place of the 150/180 hp 8A, although as with the original powerplant, the new engine would also suffer from reliability problems. These did not seem to stop fighter aces adding to their scores, however. Aside from a change in engine, the SE 5a featured wing rear spars that were shortened at the tips to give the airframe improved strength overall. Royal Aircraft Factory engineers also reduced the length of the levers that operated the aileron controls, giving the aircraft better handling characteristics. Finally, a fabric-covered head fairing was added to the fuselage behind the cockpit.

The remarkable Capt J T B McCudden VC DSO and Bar MC and Bar MM claimed all but six of his 57 victories flying the SE 5/5a with No 56 Sqn in 1917-18. He had previously scored five victories in the DH 2 with No 29 Sqn in 1916–17 and a solitary Pup success with No 66 Sqn in July 1917

The cockpit and forward fuselage of an SE 5a from No 56 Sqn. Note the control column, complete with trigger mechanism. Ahead of the cockpit is a small, flat windscreen and the tube of the Aldis sight, with the fuselage-mounted Vickers gun to the left *(Bruce Robertson)*

Photographed with his dog 'Bruiser' at Turnberry, in Scotland, in 1918, Capt James McCudden was only 22 at the time of his death, yet he was the most highly decorated pilot of the RFC, RNAS and RAF in World War 1 *(Bruce Robertson)*

McCudden wrote the following diary entry just prior to joining No 56 Sqn:

'56 was in England temporarily to strafe the Gothas. I met one or two fellows I knew in the unit, in addition to (Maj G H) Bowman. There was a wonderful spirit in this squadron, which was entirely different from any squadron with which I had yet come in contact, and everyone in the squadron was as keen as anything to get at, and strafe, the Huns. 56 had the SE 5 machines, of which we thought very highly.'

McCudden was so keen to join the unit that he started flying with No 56 Sqn while still serving with No 66 Sqn! He noted details of his first flight in the following diary entry;

'We crossed the lines at 16,000 ft over Dixmude. This was the first time I had ever been in an SE 5, and although it felt rather strange, I liked the machine immensely, as it was very fast after the Sopwith Scout (Pup), and one could see out of it so thoroughly well.'

His patrol then got into a scrap with several Albatros scouts;

'Directly we arrived over Houthulst Forest, down went the leader at a terrific speed, and I was left a long way behind. However, I got down to them again and assisted in putting the draught up some V-strutters (Albatros scouts). After this, I lost the leader and then met (Lt A P F) Rhys Davids, so together we went towards about eight V-strutters who were above us over Polygon Wood, and the next thing I saw Rhys Davids' SE absolutely standing on its tail, spitting bullets up at the Huns above him. Several of them at once came down on him, and the nearest one was so engrossed in chasing Rhys Davids that he did not see me until I had got in a good burst at close range, after which the Hun turned and flew east for a little way, and then he started to go down in a steep side-slipping spiral, apparently out of control.'

Once McCudden had joined No 56 Sqn full-time, he reflected on his new mount;

'The SE 5 was a most efficient fighting machine – far and away superior to the enemy machines of that period. It had a Vickers gun shooting forward through the propeller and a Lewis gun shooting forward over the top plane, parallel to the Vickers, but above the propeller. The pilot could also incline the Lewis gun upwards in such a way that he could shoot vertically upwards at a target that presented itself.

'Other good points of the SE 5 were its strength, its diving and zooming powers and its splendid view. Apart from this, it was most warm, comfortable and an easy machine to fly.'

Through the second half of 1917 and during the first two months of 1918, McCudden increased his score to 57 victories, of which no fewer than 21 were brought down inside Allied lines, thus leaving no doubt as to their certainty. His country bestowed upon him the DSO and Bar,

This Rumpler C V aircraft was shot down at Marzingarbe by Capt James McCudden for his 18th victory at 1300 hrs on 21 October 1917 *(Bruce Robertson)*

In February 1918 Capt McCudden fitted the four-blade propeller of his SE 5a (B8491 'G') with the spinner from an LVG C V two-seater that he had shot down on 30 November 1917. This particular airframe was the most successful SE 5a ever built in terms of aerial victories, for McCudden claimed 31 successes with it and Maj Crowe two *(Bruce Robertson)*

as well as a Bar to his MC. And on 2 April 1918 the announcement of McCudden's well-deserved VC was made, the following citation to accompany the medal being published in that day's *London Gazette*;

'For most conspicuous bravery, exceptional perseverance and a very high devotion to duty. Capt McCudden has at the present time accounted for 54 enemy aeroplanes. Of these, 42 have been destroyed, 19 of them on our side of the lines. Only 12 out of the 54 have been driven down out of control. On two occasions, he had totally destroyed four two-seater enemy aeroplanes on the same day, and on the last occasion all four machines were destroyed in the space of just one hour and thirty minutes.

'While in his present squadron, he has participated in 78 offensive patrols, and in nearly every case has been the leader. On at least 30 occasions, whilst with the same squadron, he has crossed the lines alone, either in pursuit or in quest of enemy aeroplanes.

'The following incidents are examples of the work he has done recently. On 23 December 1917, when leading his patrol, eight enemy aeroplanes were attacked between 1430/1550 hrs, and of these, two were shot down by Capt McCudden in our lines. On the morning of the same day, he left the ground at 1050 hrs and encountered four enemy aeroplanes. Of these, he shot two down. On 30 January 1918, he, single-handed, attacked five enemy scouts, as a result of which two were destroyed. On this occasion,

he only returned home when the enemy scouts had been driven far east – his Lewis gun ammunition was all finished, and the belt of his Vickers gun had broken.

'As a patrol leader, he has at all times shown the utmost gallantry and skill, not only in the manner in which he has attacked and destroyed the enemy, but in the way he has, during several aerial fights, protected the newer members of his flight, thus keeping down their casualties to a minimum. This officer is considered, by the record he has made, by his fearlessness and by the great service which he has rendered to his country, deserving of the very highest honour.'

Ending his time with No 56 Sqn in the early spring, McCudden returned home for a rest, before being given command of SE 5a-equipped No 60 Sqn in July. Having survived more than 100 offensive patrols, he was tragically killed in a flying accident at Marquise, in France, on 9 July 1918 when on his way to join his new unit at Boffles. Mistakenly landing at the wrong airfield, McCudden's engine failed shortly after take-off, possibly due to an incorrectly installed carburettor, and the fighter crashed. The ace's remains were duly buried nearby at Wavans War Cemetery in the Pas de Calais.

Capt Cecil Lewis claimed his eight victories while flying with No 56 Sqn alongside Maj McCudden, and despite the reservations he expressed earlier in this chapter about the SE 5, he praised the scout in his book *Farewell to Wings*;

'By the summer of 1917, the SE 5 was a formidable opponent for any German fighter. It could be dived to terminal velocity without breaking up. It had no vices, and would spin left and right without being difficult to pull out, as some other aircraft were. It was easy to land and had a broad, strong undercarriage.

'The SE 5 was probably the first fighting aircraft to be produced which was both reliable enough and steady enough to stand up to the rough and tumble of 30 or 40 aircraft milling around trying to shoot each other down. In such conditions, pilots did not think much about "handling". They were pretty rough on the controls. Slammed into a dive, yanked into a climb, pulled hard round in a split-arse turn, the aircraft structure had to stand up to enormous and sudden strains. The SE 5 came through this ordeal triumphantly, and justified the belief of the top brass that it would give the Allies the supremacy of the air in 1917. It did.'

A rear view of Capt McCudden's high-scoring SE 5a B4891 'G'. This photograph was almost certainly taken at Baizieux in early 1918

Claiming eight victories with the SE 5 in May-June 1917, Lt C A Lewis MC of No 56 Sqn gained lasting fame post-war as author of the aviation classic *Sagittarius Rising*. One of the founders of BBC Radio, Lewis also received an Oscar (along with George Bernard Shaw, Ian Dalrymple and W P Lipscomb) at the 1938 Academy Awards ceremony, for his screen adaptation of *Pygmalion*

In 1918 No 56 Sqn continued to produce aces, but with smaller overall scores. The leading pilot of this period was Canadian H J 'Hank' Burden DSO DFC, who would later become the brother-in-law of controversial ace Maj W A 'Billy' Bishop. He scored 16 victories between March and August, including five on 10 August and three more two days later! All but three of his tally was scored in C1096. Surviving the war, Burden passed away on 28 March 1960 – one month prior to his 67th birthday.

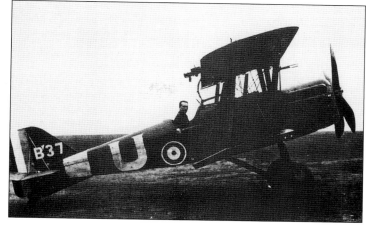

No 56 Sqn's Capt W S Fielding-Johnson MC claimed six victories in SE 5a B37 in February-March 1918 (E F Cheesman)

Fellow Canadian Capt Ken Junor from Toronto received the MC in the early weeks of 1918 after downing eight aircraft, but he was killed in action on 23 April by nine-victory ace Egon Koepsch of *Jasta* 4. Junor was just 23 when he died.

The third Canadian to achieve ace status with No 56 Sqn in 1918 was Capt William R Irwin, who scored 11 victories during the course of 70 patrols. Hailing from Ripley, Ontario, he joined the unit just prior to his 20th birthday, and would end the war with a DFC and Bar to his credit.

The last pilot to 'make ace' with No 56 Sqn was Londoner Capt Duncan Grinnell-Milne MC, who had actually spent time as a prisoner of war (PoW) after being shot down behind enemy lines in a BE 2 in December 1915 whilst serving with No 16 Sqn. Having spent more than two years as a PoW, Grinnell-Milne succeeded in escaping back to France in April 1918. Decorated for his escape, by sleight of hand he managed to get himself sent to No 56 Sqn in the final weeks of the war and made up for lost time by claiming four aircraft and a balloon to add to one victory he had achieved in 1915. Awarded the DFC and Bar, Grinnell-Milne eventually took command of No 56 Sqn in December 1918 at just 22 years of age.

Canadian Capt H J 'Hank' Burden DSO DFC claimed 16 victories with No 56 Sqn in 1918, 11 of which were scored in August alone. His greatest day came on 10 August, when he destroyed five Fokker D VIIs in C1096 during the course of two patrols

No 56 Sqn had flown the SE 5/5a for longer than any other unit in World War 1, and no fewer than 26 pilots had achieved five or more victories with the fighter. Only No 84 came close to matching this figure, with 24 aces. No 56 Sqn eventually replaced its SE 5as with Sopwith Snipes in February 1920.

No 60 Sqn
RECEIVES SE 5s

The second unit to be issued with SE 5s was No 60 Sqn, which exchanged its Nieuport 17s and 23s for the new fighting scout at

Fellow Canadian Capt K W Junor MC had destroyed eight aircraft by the time he was shot down and killed by nine-victory ace Egon Koepsch of *Jasta* 4 on 23 April 1918. Note the name *BUBBLY KID II* painted on the nose of his SE 5a C1086, in which he claimed his final three victories (*via Bob Lynes*)

Capt Junor's C1086 'E' is worked
on at No 56 Sqn's Valheureux base
in the early spring of 1918
(*via Bob Lynes*)

No 60 Sqn SE 5 B507 was captured
on 5 October 1917 when it was
forced down on *Jasta* 18's airfield.
Previously a No 56 Sqn machine,
it had been used by 20-victory ace
Lt L M Barlow to claim seven of
his successes in July-August 1917.
Fellow ace Lt Rhys Davids had also
occasionally flown B507, but had
not achieved any victories with it
(*L A Rogers*)

Filescamp Farm, west of Arras, in June 1917. A total of 17 aces would
be created by the unit with the SE5/5a, with the highest scorer being
Canadian Capt Frank O 'Mongoose' Soden DFC. Although born in
Petitcodiac, New Brunswick, in November 1895, he had lived with his
family in England since 1904. Soden had claimed his first two victories
flying Nieuport 17s with No 60 Sqn in June and July 1917, his unit
continuing to use the French fighter until August of that year when it
received the last of its SE 5as.

Soden would fly 159 patrols and claim 14 victories with the SE 5
during his time with No 60 Sqn. He then moved to No 41 Sqn as a flight
commander and increased his score to 27, winning the DFC. Remaining
in the RAF post-war, Soden was awarded a Bar to this decoration in Iraq
in 1922. Commanding RAF Biggin Hill during the early stages of World
War 2, he passed away in 1961.

Hailing from Guildford, in Western Australia, 21-year-old Capt
Harold A Hamersley MC was the second-ranking SE 5 ace within No 60
Sqn, claiming 13 victories. He had previously served as a commissioned
officer in the Australian Imperial Force, seeing action at Gallipoli in
1915. Transferring to the RFC, Hamersley was posted to No 60 Sqn in
September 1917 and claimed his first two victories on the 16th and 22nd

of that same month. The young Australian was lucky to survive his third combat, on 23 September, for his SE 5a was badly damaged by 48-victory ace Werner Voss, who was in turn shot down and killed minutes later by No 56 Sqn ace Lt A P F Rhys Davids.

Promoted to captain and awarded the MC in early 1918, Hamersley claimed his final three victories on 30 March whilst flying SE 5a C5385. He then returned to England. Hamersley rejoined No 60 Sqn in Risalpur, in northern India, in 1920, by which time its SE 5as had long since been replaced by DH 9As and DH 10s. Made CO of the squadron whilst in India, Hamersley subsequently spent time as a test pilot with A V Roe & Co Ltd. Station commander at RAF Hullavington in 1940, he passed away in December 1967.

Capt James D Belgrave MC, from Sandown, on the Isle of Wight, was No 60 Sqn's third-ranking ace with 12 victories. Born in Kensington, London, in 1896, he had already enjoyed an eventful war prior to being posted to the SE 5 unit. Initially serving with the Ox and Bucks Light

Capt F O 'Mongoose' Soden DFC was No 60 Sqn's leading SE 5a ace with 14 victories. Posted to No 41 Sqn as a flight commander in August 1918, he had claimed a further 11 successes with the unit by war's end

Left
Capt J D Belgrave MC of No 60 Sqn scored 12 victories with the SE 5a prior to being killed in action on 13 June 1918

Infantry, Belgrave had been gassed and blown up in the trenches during the Battle of Loos in September 1915. Moving to the RFC after recovering from his wounds, Belgrave flew Sopwith 1½ Strutters with No 45 Sqn in the early months of 1917. During this time he gained no fewer than six victories with his various observers, receiving the MC for his efforts.

Belgrave joined No 60 Sqn at Boffles in April 1918, and quickly claimed an additional 12 victories with the SE 5a prior to his death in action on 13 June. His last seven claims came in SE 5a D5988, and he was also killed in this machine.

Capt A W Saunders DFC also scored 12 victories in SE 5as whilst serving with No 60 Sqn in 1918
(*E F Cheesman*)

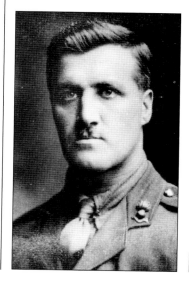

Dubliner Capt Alfred W Saunders DFC also claimed 12 victories with No 60 Sqn in 1918. Already 30 years old when he joined the unit, he was appreciably older than most of his fellow pilots in the squadron at the time. Like Hamersley and Belgrave, Saunders had seen prior action on the ground – he had served with the Royal Field Artillery in the Dardanelles. By July 1918 Saunders was commanding A Flight, and when his tour ended in early August his tally stood at 12 victories, and he had been awarded the DFC.

Three pilots claimed 11 victories with No 60 Sqn, namely Capts Alexander Beck DFC, William J A Duncan DFC MC and Bar and William A 'Billy' Bishop VC DSO and Bar MC DFC CdG Ld'H. The latter individual was the most controversial ace of World War 1, at least on the Allied side, for the majority of his 72 victories were made in circumstances where independent corroboration by witnesses was simply not available.

Born in Owen Sound, Ontario, Canada, in February 1894, Bishop had been sent to France with the Canadian Mounted Rifles at the outbreak of

Keen to do his part in securing an Allied victory, Alexander Beck had dropped out of school to join the RFC. Having lied about his age (he was born in November 1898), Beck was posted to No 60 Sqn in July 1917. After flying 13 sorties over the frontlines, his parents informed the RFC of his true age, and Beck was immediately recalled from France! Once deemed to be old enough for combat, he returned to No 60 Sqn in March 1918. Beck claimed 11 victories in the second half of 1918, including No 60 Sqn's final success of the war – a Fokker D VII, downed near Mormal Woods at 1600 hrs on 1 November 1918

World War 1. Transferring to the RFC in July 1915, he had initially served as an observer with RE 7-equipped No 21 Sqn. Undertaking pilot training in 1916-17, Bishop joined No 60 Sqn in March 1917. Attaining ace status on 5 April, he had claimed no fewer than 36 victories with Nieuport scouts by the time he made the switch to the SE 5 in mid July. A further 11 successes were credited to the Canadian ace prior to his tour ending in mid August 1917. Bishop would subsequently enjoy even greater success in the SE 5a whilst leading No 85 Sqn in 1918, as detailed in Chapter 3.

The exploits of Anglo-Argentine Alexander Beck are less well known by comparison. Born in November 1898, his family originated from Cumbria. Once in England, Beck had trained to become a pilot, and joined No 60 Sqn in July 1917. However, once his family learnt of this, and reported that he was under age, he was hastily sent back to England. If Beck's recorded birth date is indeed correct, the 18-year-old fighter pilot had already completed 13 war patrols prior to his premature removal from France! Once 'older', Beck returned to No 60 Sqn in 1918 and claimed 11 victories – the last of these was a Fokker D VII downed just ten days before the Armistice.

Fellow ace William Duncan, from Toronto, Ontario, was of sufficient age to be a fighter pilot, having been born in July 1891. After serving with Canadian forces in France, he joined the RFC, and is always mentioned as having a 'roving commission' with No 60 Sqn, without this term being fully explained. Roving or otherwise, Duncan was clearly a talented pilot, for he scored 11 victories between November 1917 and June 1918. Post-war, he became a leading professional hockey player in Canada, and lived until 1975.

Fellow SE 5 ace Lt William E Jenkins from Rushden, in Northamptonshire, celebrated his 19th birthday with No 60 Sqn on 8 July 1917, having scored four of his ten victories by this date. He served with Capt Keith Caldwell's A Flight (see the No 74 Sqn section for Caldwell's details) throughout his time with No 60 Sqn, claiming his tenth victory on 19 November. Sadly, Jenkins was not to see his 20th birthday, for he collided with another SE 5a whilst on patrol on 23 November, and both pilots fell to their deaths.

The scores of the remaining nine pilots to claim five or more victories flying SE 5/5as with No 60 Sqn are recorded in the appendices. Amongst their number is nine-victory ace Capt John E Doyle DFC from Somerset, who provided details of his last aerial engagement in an article published in *Popular Flying* magazine in the 1930s. Doyle's promising career as a fighter pilot was cut short on 5 September 1918 when he became yet another SE 5a ace to fall victim to ace Egon Koepsch of *Jasta* 4. Escorting DH 4s on a bombing raid, Doyle and his charges had attacked their target and were heading home when a gaggle of Fokker D VIIs appeared below them. Eager to claim his tenth victory, Doyle quickly decided to bounce them;

'I closed my radiator shutter and rocked my machine slowly to attract the attention of my patrol. I wound my tail-wheel (elevator control) forward and held the bus up with the stick while I watched the Fokkers' progress with interest. Then I saw some tracer leave the leading Fokker. At that moment a red Very light curved into the sky from one of the DH 4s. This was clearly my summons, but I hoped it would not cause the Huns to look round.

'I let my stick go forward and my bus dropped from under me. I looked back. With one exception, my patrol appeared to be unaware that I was diving, for they remained above. The exception, Lt (J W) Rayner, was close on my right. Soon we were down behind the Fokkers, and rushing at them, we had the two rear machines of that formation of five in our sights.

'We held our fire until the last possible minute, then opened up simultaneously. I can clearly recall being aware that tracer left Rayner's guns at the same instant that I pressed my own triggers. I was also aware of a sheet of flame in the cockpit of the right-hand Fokker. My own target shot up vertically and stalled.

'Being very close to my man when he reared up, I had to shoot my stick forward and pass below him. I was still travelling very fast, and that put me in a dive again. I got the leader in my sight and let go another burst. This time the Fokker did a flick left turn and dived in a southerly direction. Already, I had turned south and was diving after my man. There were two more Fokkers about, but I thought that they would be well marked. I got in another burst and held it while I tried to close up, but the only result was that my man went into a still steeper dive, always flying straight, so I knew I had got him.

'But the laugh was on me also, for a burst of close range stuff crashed into my SE at that moment. A bullet cracked past just clear of the cockpit, a second went through the instrument board into the tank and the third struck my head just behind the ear and cut the buckle off my chin strap, which fell slowly down. Two more cracks and then a terrific concussion. I was pressed against the side of the cockpit, unable to move, while the aeroplane fell headlong, turning on its axis as it did so. Petrol was pouring on me, and I managed to depress the switch.

'I looked down into the cockpit and saw that my right flying boot had been folded back, but with the foot still in the stirrup. That concussion I had experienced had been due to a bullet smashing my shinbone, and at the same time paralysing the nerve. I grabbed the boot and dragged it out of the stirrup, then pulled it with my left leg, and the aeroplane responded immediately. I looked up past my tail and got a head-on impression of two Fokkers diving at me. The ground was near, but I dived again to maintain my lead, flattened out hurriedly and made a landing of sorts in what appeared to be a park.'

Capt John Doyle's war was over, for his wound was so bad that he subsequently lost his right leg whilst a PoW.

No 84 SQN

Flying a variety of British, French and American aircraft types following it formation at Beaulieu, in Hampshire, in January 1917, No 84 Sqn converted onto SE 5as at Lilbourne, in Northamptonshire, in August 1917. The unit moved to Liettres, south of St-Omer, the following month, and remained in France until after Armistice Day.

A total of 24 pilots would attain ace status with the squadron by war's end, with diminutive South African (he was just over five foot tall) Anthony Frederick Weatherby Proctor – to which he added Beauchamp

The SE 5/5a 'ace of aces', South African Capt A F W Beauchamp Proctor VC DSO DFC claimed no fewer than 54 victories with No 84 Sqn in 1918

as suggested by his father when he left to join up – being by far and away its top scorer with 54 victories.

Born on 4 September 1894, Beauchamp Proctor left the University of Cape Town to join the Duke of Edinburgh's Own Rifles. He duly served with the unit in German South-West Africa in 1914, but returned to university to complete his studies the following year. Recruited into the RFC in March 1917, Beauchamp Proctor travelled to England to train as a pilot, and eventually joined No 84 Sqn just as the unit received the first of its SE 5as in late July. Heading to France with the squadron, he failed to score his first victory until 3 January 1918.

Due to his modest height, Beauchamp Proctor had had to have the seat fitted in his fighter adjusted so that he could reach the rudder pedals – the latter were also specially lengthened.

Despite his low-key start in terms of aerial successes, Beauchamp Proctor quickly hit his straps from February onwards. For example, on 17 March he downed three aircraft to boost his tally to nine – he was awarded the MC following this action. By mid June Beauchamp Proctor had claimed 12 aircraft and four kite balloons destroyed, and 12 more aircraft sent down out of control. Posted back to England for a rest at the end of that month, the South African was awarded one of the first DFCs in July – this medal had been instituted by Royal Warrant as recently as 3 June 1918.

Returning to No 84 Sqn in August, Beauchamp Proctor continued to add to his tally of victories until suffering severe wounds in his forearm on 8 October. Indeed, he was so badly injured that he remained in hospital until March 1919. His final tally stood at 54 victories, of which 16 were tethered observation kite balloons. The latter were considered by many pilots to be the most dangerous targets on the Western Front, as they were usually surrounded by a cordon of anti-aircraft guns and fighters (see *Osprey Aircraft of the Aces 66 – Balloon-Busting Aces of World War 1* for further details).

Beauchamp Proctor had used five SE 5as during distinct scoring periods in 1918. His first five victories had been achieved in B539, followed by four in D259, ten in C1772 and nine in D333. No fewer than 16 victories were claimed in D6856, after which Beauchamp Proctor was assigned C1911 – he claimed nine of his final ten successes in this machine.

The RFC/RAF's leading balloon-buster, Beauchamp Proctor received the DSO and VC whilst convalescing in hospital. Once he had recovered from his wounds, the SE 5a 'ace of aces' made an extensive tour of the US, before returning home to South Africa in February 1920. Beauchamp Proctor was back in England by the end of the year, and after attending the RAF College at Cranwell, he was granted a permanent commission. He joined No 24 Sqn shortly afterwards, and on 21 June 1921 Beauchamp Proctor was killed in a flying accident at Upavon whilst practising aerobatics in a Sopwith Snipe for the forthcoming Hendon Air Pageant.

A F W Beauchamp Proctor so dominated No 84 Sqn's victory tally that the unit's second-ranking ace, Capt Walter A Southey DFC and Bar, scored some 34 fewer successes than the diminutive South African. Born in Bermondsey, south London, in April 1897, Southey was living in

South Africa when war broke out in Europe. Returning to the UK, he initially joined the 19th Royal Fusiliers in February 1916, prior to transferring to the RFC.

Posted to Bristol F 2A Fighter-equipped No 48 Sqn at La Bellevue, west of Arras, Southey was shot down and wounded on 4 June 1917. Out of action until March 1918, he joined No 84 Sqn at Flez and subsequently claimed 20 victories, including a run of five observation kite balloons in September-October. Southey received a DFC and Bar for his successes both in the air and against German troops on the ground, as the following citation (which appeared in the *London Gazette* on 2 November 1918) accompanying these awards alludes to;

'A gallant and skilful officer, on 9 August, observing a large body of enemy troops and artillery on a road, he descended to 50 ft and bombed them, causing heavy casualties. He then engaged them with machine gun fire, inflicting further loss and scattering them in all directions. He also displays great courage in the air, having accounted for seven enemy aircraft.'

Southey was transferred out of No 84 Sqn one week after Armistice Day, and like fellow ace A F W Beauchamp Proctor, he did not live long to enjoy peace, being killed in an accident on 17 April 1920.

Third in the list of No 84 Sqn aces is Capt Carl F Falkenberg DFC and Bar with 17 victories. Born in Newfoundland in February 1897, he initially served with the Quebec Regiment, prior to joining the RFC. As with Beauchamp Proctor and Southey, Falkenberg really hit his straps between April and October 1918. Unlike his two ace companions, however, he lived to the ripe old age of 83, before passing away in Edmonton, Canada.

Capts Robert A 'Robin' Grosvenor MC and Bar and Sidney W Highwood DFC and Bar both scored 16 victories with No 84 Sqn. Grosvenor, who was the son of Lord and Lady Grosvenor of Chester, was born in May 1895 and commissioned into the 2nd Dragoon Guards soon after World War 1 commenced. Eventually switching to the RFC, Grosvenor's successes with No 84 Sqn brought him the MC and Bar, and command of A Flight until the late spring of 1918 – he used SE 5a B8408 to claim the last 11 of his 16 victories. Grosvenor died in June 1953.

Born in Marden, Kent, in December 1896, Sid Highwood was another No 84 Sqn ace who enjoyed hunting kite balloons. Often flying with Beauchamp Proctor, Southey and Falkenberg, he claimed nine balloons destroyed as part of his tally of 16 victories, including three on 24 September and two more five days later.

Capt Hugh William Lumsden Saunders DFC MC was yet another South African to attain ace status with No 84 Sqn, ending the war with 15 victories to his credit. Having already won the MM with the South African Horse, Saunders (nicknamed 'Dingbat') transferred to the RFC and joined No 84 Sqn at Le Hameau in November 1917 following his pilot training. Also enjoying success throughout 1918, Saunders remained in the RAF post-war, and eventually earned a Bar to his DFC in 1921 for services in Mesopotamia – primarily for dropping supplies to a beleaguered British garrison and to a gunboat. Air Officer Commanding (AOC) No 11 Group, RAF Fighter Command, between 1942-44, Saunders achieved high rank and was knighted for his services. Also

Capt C F Falkenberg DFC and Bar achieved 17 victories with No 84 Sqn in 1918, leading the unit's B Flight in the last two months of the war. Upon his return to England soon after Armistice Day, Falkenberg transferred to the Royal Canadian Air Force and served as a flight commander with No 1 Sqn until his discharge on 18 October 1919

Capt R A Grosvenor MC and Bar was No 84 Sqn's fourth-ranking SE 5a ace with 16 victories (*E F Cheesman*)

briefly serving as Air Officer Commander-in-Chief Bomber Command post-World War 2, he eventually retired as Air Marshal Saunders GCB KCB and died on 8 May 1987.

More than 30 years ago, I was in correspondence with No 84 Sqn ace Capt Graeme Leask MC and Bar, who had claimed eight victories with the unit. Born in Southsea, Hampshire, in October 1896, he had seen service in the Devonshire

Enjoying time away from the front whilst instructing at Turnberry in 1918, these pilots are, from left to right, Capt J V Sorsoleil MC of No 84 Sqn (14 victories), Capt H W L Saunders MC DFC MM also of No 84 Sqn (15 victories), Capt R W Chappell MC of No 41 Sqn (11 victories, 9 with the SE 5a), Lt Yuill MC and Capt P J Clayson MC DFC of No 1 Sqn (29 victories)

Regiment and the Machine Gun Corps, prior to undertaking RFC pilot training. Leask flew Royal Aircraft Factory BE 2s with No 42 Sqn and then Royal Aircraft Factory FE 8s with No 41 Sqn before joining No 84 Sqn and eventually serving as a flight commander.

Claiming all of his victories between October 1917 and March 1918, Leask recalled what it was like to fly in combat over the Western Front during this period of the war;

'It was quite normal to be outnumbered by at least two-to-one, and in consequence we suffered losses – chiefly due to inexperience, and a failure by pilots to keep formation, rather than going off chasing after Huns. In the excitement of the moment, and in the eagerness to get a Hun, the young pilot would forget about sticking to his leader and go down after the enemy.

'On one occasion, having maintained my height, I found myself being given the works by six Fokker triplanes, which were more manoeuvrable than the SE 5, and they came down from the sun. I received a real thrashing.

'I had two main spars shot about, my gravity tank in the centre section was holed and petrol was spraying back over my head. One of the bullets in that group had been a phosphorus round, which had set the fabric smouldering just a few inches away from the leaking petrol tank. My SE 5 was full of holes, and even the axle was shot through, but I had a charmed life.

'During an escort for DH 4s of 5 Naval Squadron one day, we were at 18,000 ft and had a height advantage over the Huns who came up in swarms to attack the bombers. We swooped down and attacked with good results, and the thing developed into an enormous dogfight. We were about 20 miles over the lines, and I had just made one successful attack when, to my horror, my engine started to cut out and fade. Realising I had carburettor trouble, I glided out of the fight without being spotted. The wing loading of the SE 5 was very small, and therefore the take-off run was short and the gliding angle shallow – about 1000 ft of altitude to one mile, if there was no adverse wind. I was lucky to get back over the lines.

'I think it essential to mention the importance of marksmanship, without which there could be no victories. Without boasting, I was a crack shot with a rifle or machine gun, and had been so since school, where I won the shooting cup three times running. I shot down two enemy aircraft on our side of the lines. One was a DFW, and the pilot

No 84 Sqn's Capt K M StC G Leask MC and Bar was credited with eight victories

was twice hit in the head and five times in the body. The other was a scout, shot down during the Battle of Cambrai. My Vickers gun had jammed after three rounds, and the pilot went straight down and landed. We did not get the machine in, as the battle was raging to and fro, but it was confirmed by two members of my patrol, as well as ground forces.

'Most of my patrols with No 84 Sqn were made in SE 5a B637 – I flew 99 sorties in this aircraft between 12 November 1917 and 1 April 1918 (five of Leask's victories came whilst flying this machine). My first two SE 5as were B4874 and B579, and they were both subsequently crashed by other pilots.'

Graeme Leask's 'charmed life' ended tragically in a car accident on 24 April 1974, in which both he and his wife were killed. He had retired from the RAF 25 years earlier as an air vice-marshal.

Another notable ace to serve with No 84 Sqn was Lt John 'Jack' Anthony McCudden MC, younger brother of famous No 56 Sqn ace Maj James McCudden. John was born in June 1897, and like his brother, he had joined the Royal Engineers in 1912. He was sent to France in 1914 as a despatch rider, and eventually volunteered for the RFC after seeing the success that the switch had brought his older sibling. Once a pilot, John joined No 25 Sqn in September 1917, and quickly saw action in the unit's DH 4 bombers. He and his gunners claimed two victories within weeks of arriving in the frontline, and McCudden was transferred to No 84 Sqn before the end of the year. Having achieved six more victories, he became the first of ten victims for Hans Joachim Wolff of *Jasta* 11 on 18 March 1918.

Many years later, 15-victory ace Hugh Saunders, mentioned previously in this chapter, recalled the younger McCudden for me;

'"Jack" McCudden lived in the shadow of his elder brother, and was too anxious to emulate him. As an extremely gallant young pilot, in the short time that he was with the squadron he destroyed a number of enemy aircraft and was awarded the MC. He was, however, too impetuous and aggressive to last long, and was shot down and killed in March 1918. A great loss, but an inevitable end for a pilot who was always prepared to take on any odds.'

No 84 Sqn was commanded by Maj W A Sholto-Douglas MC (later C-in-C of RAF Fighter Command in World War 2) from August 1917 to November 1918, and he had the following to say about his unit's employment of the SE 5a during this period;

'When we saw enemy aircraft approaching, we would climb as hard as we could – if possible up into the sun – and then we would try to take them from above and behind, out of the sun. The superior performance of our SE 5s enabled us to do this more or less with impunity.

'On occasions I did manage to get my SE 5 up to a height of just over 22,000 ft by pushing the aircraft hard – usually in order to get into a position from which I could dive down unseen on the Hun. That was not possible with rotary-engined machines such as the 1¹/₂ Strutter or the Camel, and even the SE 5 became sluggish and difficult to control, and only too ready to fall out of one's hands, at this height. Any exertion at such an altitude without oxygen left one gasping for breath, but that, and the cold, were the only discomforts I ever suffered.'

American 1Lt George A Vaughn Jr DFC DSC(US) flew Camels with the USAS's 17th Aero Squadron after seeing action in SE 5as with the RAF's No 84 Sqn in 1918. He became an ace with both units, totting up 13 victories overall (*Bruce Robertson*)

THE SE 5a IS ESTABLISHED

The RFC began equipping its fourth fighter unit with SE 5as in mid October 1917, No 40 Sqn having already made a name for itself by then with the FE 8 pusher scout and then Nieuport 17/23/24 Scouts. The unit had been in France since August 1916, and its period with the Nieuports, in particular, often appears in history books about the RFC, for No 40 Sqn had a good record of success with the aircraft thanks to a handful of exceptional pilots. Not the least of these was Capt Edward 'Mick' Mannock (15 victories), who served with the unit during his embryonic days as a tyro pilot. His pals Lt William MacLanachan (seven victories) and Capts Arthur W Keen (11 victories), Albert E Godfrey and John H Tudhope (two victories) also played their part.

When No 40 Sqn re-equipped with the SE 5a, a whole new chapter began in the unit's history, and its leading light was Capt G E H 'McIrish' McElroy MC and two Bars DFC and Bar. George McElroy's time with the unit was split by an eight-week spell as a flight commander with No 24 Sqn in March-April 1918. Born in Donnybrook, near Dublin, on 14 May 1893, he had joined the Royal Irish Regiment in 1914 and been commissioned in May of the following year. Badly gassed in France, McElroy was sent home to perform garrison duty, but he was eager to return to the fighting so volunteered for the RFC in February 1917.

The future ace joined No 40 Sqn at Bruay, west of Lens, just as the Nieuport was ending its days with the unit, and McElroy only began to score once flying the SE 5a. During his first weeks in the squadron he was tutored by Capt 'Mick' Mannock, and the advice the latter pilot gave McElroy was put to good use by the Irishman between December 1917

Capt J H Tudhope MC and Bar of No 40 Sqn scored the last two of his eight SE 5a victories in B189 'S' on 10 and 11 April 1918, while 12-victory ace Capt Bill Harrison also claimed one (on 26 March 1918) (*L A Rogers*)

In two periods with No 40 Sqn, Capt G E H McElroy MC and two Bars, DFC and Bar (right) scored 31 of his 47 SE 5a victories. He is seen here with fellow No 40 Sqn ace Capt G H Lewis DFC, who claimed 12 victories – ten with SE 5as and two with DH 2s

and mid-February 1918, when he scored 11 victories.

McElroy was then posted to Matigny-based No 24 Sqn as a flight commander, and with this unit he claimed 16 victories in just eight weeks. The last three of these came during a single patrol on 7 April, although he crashed into a tree upon landing at No 24 Sqn's Conteville base at the end of the patrol and was badly shaken. Prevented from flying for two months due to his injuries, McElroy returned to action with No 40 Sqn (now at Bryas) in June. Renowned for being an aggressive dogfighter who routinely ignored often-overwhelming odds, he added to his score almost daily in July.

On 20 July No 40 Sqn held a farewell dinner to 12-victory ace Capt G H Lewis DFC, and Maj 'Mick' Mannock, now CO of No 85 Sqn, was one of the invited guests who flew over to Bruay for the event. During the function, McElroy and Mannock both admonished each other for being too aggressive, and for flying too low in pursuit of victories. Six days later Mannock was killed doing just that, while McElroy fell in similar circumstances less than a week afterwards, on 31 July. It seems McElroy had just shot down a German two-seater when his SE 5a was struck by ground fire. This final victory went unclaimed.

Capt McElroy's last two confirmed successes (taking his official tally to 47) were Hannover CL machines on the morning of 25 July, and his combat report for this date noted;

'I singled out one of two Hannovers patrolling west of Bois de Biez and dived down from in front of the enemy aircraft unobserved. I fired a burst of 100 rounds at 200 yards range from the front and zoomed off. On preparing to dive underneath, I saw an enemy aircraft falling out of control, slowly spinning until it finally crashed north of Neuve Capelle.

'I then observed an enemy aircraft over Mettallique Works. I flew east of the enemy aircraft and dived down from its right rear, firing a few short bursts at fairly close range, but had to pull off owing to fuel pressure trouble. Having changed over to my emergency tank, I then followed the enemy aircraft, which was now heading east. I secured a position behind the tail of the enemy aircraft and fired 100 rounds from 200 yards down to 100 yards range. The enemy aircraft went into a steep dive, pulled out temporarily at about 1000 ft, but then seemed to stall and spin, before finally crashing just west of Bois D'Epinoy.'

Lt Louis Bennett Jr was No 24 Sqn second-ranking SE 5a ace with 12 victories. Born to a wealthy, politically prominent family in Weston, West Virginia, on 22 September 1894, Bennett had graduated from Yale

West Virginian Lt Louis Bennett Jr was one of two pilots to claim 12 victories flying SE 5as with No 40 Sqn. These successes were achieved in the space of just ten days between 15 and 24 August 1918. Nine of Bennett's victims were kite balloons (*E F Cheesman*)

Maj Reed Landis is seen here wearing his early DFC ribbon, won for the 12 victories he claimed between May and mid-August 1918 while flying SE 5as with No 40 Sqn. He ended the war commanding the USAS's 25th Pursuit Squadron (*Bruce Robertson*)

and joined the RFC in Canada in early 1917. Following flying training in Texas and the UK, he graduated on 6 March 1918 and was assigned to Sopwith Dolphin-equipped No 90 Sqn at Shotwick, in Cheshire. This unit was performing home defence duties, and Bennett was keen to see action in France, so he eventually obtained a posting to No 40 Sqn.

Arriving at Bryas on 21 July, Bennett was assigned to 'McIrish' McElroy's C Flight, but the latter pilot was killed whilst leading the American's second patrol. It took a month for Bennett to find his feet, but then, amazingly, in August 1918 he claimed 12 victories in just ten days during the course of just 25 sorties with the unit. Nine of these successes were against kite balloons, four of which fell on the 19th, two more on the 22nd and another double on the 24th.

Affected by balloon 'fever', Bennett's luck ran out on this last date while heading for a third dirigible near Hantay. Ground fire from Machine Gun Detachments Nrs 920 and 921 repeatedly struck the American's SE 5a (E3947), which burst into flames and crashed. Bennett had jumped from his blazing fighter just prior to it hitting the ground, and his German captors found him lying near the wreckage of the SE 5a grievously burned, and with a serious head wound and a broken leg. Despite being rushed to the nearest field hospital at Wavrin, the ace died while being attended to by a German doctor. So rapid had been his successes that Bennett received no decoration for his bravery, save for a belated Mention in Despatches, gazetted in July 1919.

Fellow American Maj Reed G Landis DFC DSC(US) also claimed 12 victories with No 40 Sqn in 1918. Born in Ottawa, Illinois, on 17 July 1896, he had seen service on the Mexican border in 1916 as a cavalry private in the 1st Illinois Cavalry (National Guard). Transferring to the Aviation Section of the US Signal Corps, Landis completed his flying training in the UK and was then sent to No 40 Sqn to gain combat experience prior to joining the US Air Service (USAS). This he did in full measure, scoring 12 victories between May and mid-August 1918.

Landis then transferred to the USAS, where he was assigned to the 4th Fighter Group's 25th Aero Squadron, which he later commanded. He continued to fly post-war, and later became vice-president of American Airlines. A colonel in World War 2, Landis passed away in May 1975.

Continuing No 40 Sqn's North American connection, 19-year-old Canadian Capt William L 'Harry' Harrison MC and Bar of Toronto scored his first victory with the unit in a Nieuport in the summer of 1917. He followed this up with a further ten successes in SE 5as, five of which fell to the guns of C1071. One of his fellow pilots remembered that '"Harry" had the reputation of not being able to formate, and he was always seen in the air just that little bit away at the side of the Flight'.

Most of Harrison's victories came in March 1918, shortly after which he was transferred to SE 5a-equipped No 1 Sqn as a flight commander. He gained one further victory with this unit but was then badly injured when he crashed on landing at No 1 Sqn's Clairmarais home on the very day (13 April) that the squadron moved to the site from Ste-Marie-Cappel. Harrison died in the 1960s.

Among the 11 other pilots to achieve ace status with No 40 Sqn, Capt Gwilym H Lewis DFC stands out for several reasons, not the least of which was that he became one of the last World War 1 aces to pass away. Born in Birmingham in August 1897, he initially served with the Northampton Regiment before transferring to the RFC. Having got his wings, he flew DH 2s with No 32 Sqn and claimed two victories in early 1917. Following a rest in England, Lewis became a flight commander with No 40 Sqn in late 1917. Between then and July 1918, when he was again rested, Lewis achieved a further ten victories.

He recorded details pertaining to a number of his SE 5a successes in his book *Wings over the Somme*;

'I found a Hun two-seater of a new fighter type, obviously being "archied" (shot at by flak) by his own people as a spoof. (Lt C W) Usher was having a go at him on his way down, but he had to clear off. I came down on top of the brute full of gusto, quite certain that I was well backed by the remainder of my patrol, and that the Hun would soon put his nose down and go for home like all well-behaved Huns. But not a bit of it!

'There was the little observer crouching over his gun, making the usual noises, and the old pilot doing the correct thing, turning as fast as I was, and going just about as quick, too. I thought this is where the science of the game comes in, so there I sat just under his elevator, firing all the guns I could find, and pulling at everything within reach with my usual *sang-froid*. The Hun, meantime, was leading me a merry sort of dance, and mostly going east.

'Suddenly – "clackity-clackity-clack", and I looked round, and there were three dirty fat white, black and green Albatri diving on my tail. I have never been so frightened in my life. Down I went as fast as I could, and no man has gone faster, engine going like nothing on earth. Luckily, we can dive as fast as they can, so they gave it up, fearing something on top of them I expect. I crossed the lines at a few thousand feet, being "archied" out of my life. All this didn't take long, and (Lt J H F) Hambley noticed that I had disappeared, and came down for the two-seater himself. I am proud to say he destroyed the beastly thing. Nasty green brute!

'For the next half hour or so I stuck on the lines, climbing up again. I played sort of hide and seek with one or two more Huns, and as they seemed to increase in numbers, I thought someone else could do a job of work and I went home. (Capt G E H) McElroy also got a Hun – he

Capt G H Lewis poses in his SE 5a D3540 'K'. He claimed four victories with this aircraft in April-May 1918. A fifth success was credited to squadronmate Capt C O Rusden in this machine

gets Huns most days. He specialises in two-seaters, and sits up by himself and stalks them. He is a pupil of Mannock's.'

After the war, Gwilym became a successful businessman, and his last years were spent in London. I had the privilege of meeting and talking with him on a number of occasions prior to his death on 17 December 1996, aged 99. He passed away just a month before his namesake, Cecil Lewis (an eight-victory ace with No 56 Sqn), who died in January 1997, aged 98.

No record of 40 Sqn's exploits with the SE 5a would be complete without a word about its commanding officer in 1918, naval ace Maj Roderic Stanley Dallas DSO DSC and Bar. This exceptional Australian from Queensland was 26 when he joined the unit in April 1918 following a successful career with 1 Wing, Royal Naval Air Service (RNAS), and later with 1 Naval Squadron. Dallas more or less introduced the Sopwith Triplane to the Western Front (see *Osprey Aircraft of the Aces 62 - Sopwith Triplane Aces* for further details), and with this type, and the Camel and Nieuport Scout, he had claimed more than 20 victories by 1918.

Shortly after the formation of the RAF following the amalgamation of the RFC and RNAS (on 1 April 1918), Dallas was given command of No 40 Sqn, which meant a change for him not only in culture, but also in the type of aeroplane he would now be flying. He had moved from rotary Triplanes and Camels to inline-engined SE 5as, but being the exceptional pilot that he was, this did not slow Dallas down. Indeed, he remained keen to take the fight to the enemy despite having been a frontline pilot in France since December 1915. And like most other squadron commanders at this crucial stage in the war, he was under pressure from the RAF's 'senior brass' not to fly in combat for fear of him being killed in action. Experienced leaders like Dallas were invaluable to the fledgling Air Force in the spring of 1918.

Years ago I met, and had correspondence with, five-victory ace Lt H S Wolff, who flew SE 5as with No 40 Sqn during the period that Dallas was its CO. He recalled the Australian fondly, and remembering;

'One day we were alone in the Mess, chatting about things generally, and our SE 5s in particular, when Dallas suddenly said to me, "Come on, let's have a joy-ride together". Up we went, with him leading, gaining height and turning east over the lines. I formated perfectly until at

Before he was killed in a combat with three Fokker Dr Is on 19 June 1918, Australian ace Maj Roderic Stanley Dallas had amassed 32 victories while operational with the RNAS and RAF. This photograph shows Dallas in specially camouflaged SE 5a D3511, which he used to down five German aircraft in May 1918 whilst CO of No 40 Sqn. Fellow aces Capts G E H McElroy and G H Lewis also flew the aircraft, with the latter claiming his last two victories in it in July 1918 *(Bruce Robertson)*

Lt H S Wolff claimed five victories with No 40 Sqn in 1918. Note the Aldis gunsight and the off-set Vickers machine gun position of his SE 5a

about 17,000 ft my engine became "slack", and I was unable to keep level formation with him – I ended up about 100 ft below him.

'We flew on and on in an easterly direction, with nothing in sight except "Archie". This went on for some time until I began to think we'd reach Berlin! I got a bit worried, wondering whether we'd have enough petrol to get back. To my relief he eventually turned back, and we got level again and weaved our way carefully through exploding flak.

'I really think that in his mind he wanted to test out his pilots individually, and he was the type who would not ask any of his squadronmates to do anything that he would not do himself. He was completely fearless, happy in personality, cheerful and a born leader with a most likeable manner. Everyone in the unit thought the world of him.'

Dallas claimed a further nine victories with the SE 5a, taking his final tally to 32. As a successful, and highly experienced, fighter pilot, he was not shy in coming forward when it came to engaging the enemy, as this 3 May 1918 report clearly reveals;

'Flew over La Brayelle aerodrome and fired on hangars on south side of aerodrome to attract attention. Dropped a parcel with the following message inside;

'"If you won't come up here and fight, herewith one pair of boots for work on the ground, pilot's for the use of."

'Then flew in mist till a party of men had collected to examine the parcel, then two bombs were dropped, one burst being observed near target. Opened fire with both guns, firing about 100 rounds when troops scattered. General panic ensued.'

Dallas clearly chose to ignore the requests being made of him by his senior officers to stay over the Allied side of the frontline. Sadly, the brave and brash Queenslander's luck finally ran out on the morning of 1 June 1918. Having already flown a bombing mission that day, he departed Bruay alone and started patrolling overhead the forward trenches near Lievin. Possibly distracted by a decoy aircraft, Dallas was bounced by three Fokker Dr Is from *Jasta* 14, which had obviously spotted him flying just inside the British lines – he often did this so as to keep a watchful eye on his pilots while they were over hostile territory. Dallas duly became the sixth victim of *Staffelführer* Hans Werner.

One last No 40 Sqn ace must be mentioned in detail, for he was the only Indian pilot to achieve this distinction in World War 1. Indra Lal 'Laddie' Roy was born in Calcutta on 2 December 1892, and he was attending school in London when the Great War commenced. Joining the RFC in July 1917, Roy's first posting was to No 56 Sqn three months later. However, a crash due to pilot error saw him sent back to the UK for additional training, so it was not until June 1918 that he finally joined No 40 Sqn. Although he was still judged to be medically unfit at the time following his accident, Roy managed to get this decision reversed upon his arrival in the frontline.

His time came in July 1918, when he claimed ten victories in just two weeks, before falling in a fight with *Jasta* 29 on the 22nd – credited to 30-victory ace Harald Auffarth. Roy's DFC was gazetted in September. Although sometimes noted as being only 19 years old, his birth date, if correct, shows him to have been 25 when he was killed.

No 41 Sqn

Like several other SE 5a units, No 41 Sqn had also initially been equipped with pusher scouts such as the Vickers FB 5 Gunbus, DH 2 and FE 8 during the early stages of its existence. Formed at Gosport with a nucleus of personnel drawn from No 28 Sqn, the unit was posted to Abeele in October 1916, and eventually traded its FE 8s for Airco DH 5s in July 1917. Four months later, No 41 Sqn was equipped with SE 5as at its Léalvillers base. By war's end some 15 pilots had 'made ace' flying SE 5as with the unit, with two of them boasting scores in excess of 30 victories.

No 41 Sqn's ranking ace was Canadian Capt William G Claxton DSO DFC and Bar. Born in Manitoba in June 1899, and just 18 when he joined the RFC in 1917, he travelled to the UK late that year after completing his initial training in his native country. Having earned his wings, Claxton joined No 41 Sqn in France in March 1918. He quickly earned the nickname 'Dozy' because of his imperturbability under fire, the young Canadian often bringing back battle-damaged SE 5as for his mechanics to repair.

Despite his fighters being regularly shot up, Claxton's skill in aerial combat ensured that he inflicted his fair share of damage on his opponents. Indeed, he claimed 37 victories between 27 May and 13 August 1918, with 13 of these being achieved in just four days in July (including six on the 30th – four in the morning and two in the evening). The citation that accompanied the awarding of his DFC on 3 August alluded to Claxton's fearless nature in combat;

'This officer at all times shows fine courage and disregard of danger. On a recent occasion, having destroyed a hostile balloon, he pursued an enemy scout ten miles and eventually drove it down. He was then attacked by five enemy triplanes and other scouts, but managed to return to our lines, though his machine was riddled with bullets.'

Claxton's run of successes came to an end on 17 August during a fight with a large formation of Fokker D VIIs from *Jasta* 20, the Canadian suffering a head wound whilst being attacked by future five-victory ace Ltn Johannes Gildermeister – Claxton was only the German's second victim. Crash-landing behind enemy lines, he underwent emergency cranial surgery in a German military hospital and eventually recovered from his wounds. Post-war, Claxton returned home and established himself as a journalist of some repute. He died in September 1967.

Fellow high-scoring Canadian Capt Frederick R G McCall DSO DFC MC and Bar was born in Vernon, British Columbia, in December 1896. Keen to see action in World War 1, he enlisted with the 175th Overseas Battalion attached to the Canadian Expeditionary Force (CEF) in February 1916. By the end of the year he was in England, serving as a sergeant with the battalion. McCall managed to transfer to the RFC in

Canadian Capt W G Claxton DSO DFC was the leading ace of No 41 Sqn with 37 victories. His run of success came to an abrupt end on 17 August 1918 when he was shot down by future ace Ltn Johannes Gildermeister of *Jasta* 20 on 17 August 1918 – Claxton was only the German's second victory! Surviving the engagement with a serious head wound, Claxton spent several months recovering from his injuries in a German military hospital (*T Mellor-Ellis*)

March 1917, and upon completing his flying training, he was posted to Royal Aircraft Factory RE 8-equipped No 13 Sqn in France.

McCall and his observers were credited with three victories over coming months, in spite of their unit's primary function being aerial reconnaissance. Awarded the MC and Bar for his efforts, McCall was posted to No 41 Sqn in the early spring of 1918 after completing a spell of rest. He took an immediate shine to the SE 5a, claiming 32 victories between May and August. Like Claxton, McCall also scored in multiples, downing four machines on 28 June and five two days later. These successes brought him the DFC and then a DSO.

McCall was flying with Claxton on the ill-fated 17 August mission that saw the two Canadians run into a German formation they estimated to be 40 to 60 aircraft strong, and although he managed to send a Halberstadt down out of control, he could not prevent his friend from being shot down. McCall fell ill soon after this mission, and he was initially sent back to England to rest, before eventually continuing home to Canada.

The ace established McCall Aero Corporation in 1920, which carried both passengers and freight across Canada, and he later served with the RCAF in World War 2. He eventually died in January 1949, aged 52.

The third-ranking ace in No 41 Sqn was also a Canadian, Capt William Ernest Shields DFC and Bar being born in Lipton, Saskatchewan, in October 1892. Possibly a member of the CEF prior to joining the RFC in Canada, he sailed for the UK in October 1917. Shields underwent much of his flying training with No 93 Sqn at Chattis Hill, in Hampshire, prior to being posted to No 41 Sqn in March 1918.

In some ways Shields' impressive combat record was overshadowed by his fellow countrymen. Nevertheless, he scored 24 victories between June and the Armistice, including five balloons. Five of these successes came on 3 and 5 July whilst at the controls of SE 5a D3567, and his combat report for his trio of victories on the 3rd read as follows;

'While on patrol at about 1910 hrs southeast of Villers Brettonneaux at 14,500 ft, my patrol engaged 12 Pfalz Scouts. I dived on one enemy aircraft and fired two bursts of 25 rounds from each gun into it, whereupon the scout went down vertically completely out of control. One of the enemy aircraft then succeeded in getting onto my tail, so I immediately half-rolled, and it did the same as I went down. Getting onto this enemy aircraft's tail, I fired two bursts of about 50 rounds at close range. The enemy aircraft went vertically down and crashed.

'I then climbed to get height, and two more enemy aircraft followed me. As I dived upon them, they turned east and dived away. I followed and got three good bursts into one enemy aircraft, which spun, and I observed him crash in a small wood southeast of Villers-Brettoneaux.

'Engaging a fourth enemy aircraft, my Lewis gun jammed and the belt for the Vickers gun broke, so I was obliged to break off the combat. Some Camels joined in just before I left.'

Like a number of aces from both sides, Bill Shields did not live long to enjoy the peace he had so gallantly fought for. On 1 August 1921, he perished when the DH 4 he was flying crashed at High River Air Station in Alberta. Taking off on a forestry patrol, he began a climbing turn before attaining sufficient airspeed, and the heavy DH 4 side-slipped into the ground.

Capt F R McCall DSO MC DFC was the second of three high-scoring Canadian aces to serve with No 41 Sqn, claiming 32 of his 35 victories with the unit . . .

. . . and third member of the trio was Capt W E Shields DFC and Bar, who scored 24 victories with No 41 Sqn

Proving just how many pilots from the Empire were serving with the RFC/RAF in the last year of the war, the fourth ranking ace in No 41 Sqn was Australian Capt Eric J Stephens DFC. Born in Bendigo, Victoria, in September 1895, he abandoned his university studies in Western Australia and enlisted in the Australian Army in July 1915. Initially seeing service on the Northern Front in the Ypres area from June 1916, Stephens then participated in the Somme Offensive with the 4th Machine Gun Company of the 12th Brigade. Having survived ten months in the trenches, he joined the RFC in April 1917, and had earned his wings by June of that year.

Stephens proved to be a gifted pilot, and he was retained as an instructor until finally being posted to No 41 Sqn in March 1918. Although he fought throughout the German March offensive, he did not make his first victory claim until 28 June, when he shared in the destruction of a Rumpler with Canadian ace Capt McCall. A flight commander for the final months of the war, Stephens had accumulated 13 victories and won the DFC by the Armistice. Becoming a commercial pilot post-war, he flew for Australian airline Qantas and for the Kingsford Smith/Charles Ulm company Australian National Airways until it closed down in the 1930s. Stephens eventually passed away in Lae, Papua New Guinea, in January 1967.

Canadian Capt Frank O 'Mongoose' Soden was the unit's fifth ranking ace, and his biographical details are provided in the No 60 Sqn section of Chapter 1. By the time he joined No 41 Sqn in mid July 1918 as a flight commander, he already had 16 victories to his credit. A vastly experienced fighter pilot, Soden had boosted his overall tally to 27 victories by the end of October 1918.

Surprisingly, given his sustained success in combat from June 1917 until Armistice Day, Soden received no decorations during World War 1. Anomalies over awards and medals could easily fill a large book, and Soden's is a case in point. He received no reward for his victories with No 60 Sqn, and his DFC was a late one, not being shown in the *London Gazette* until February 1919. Even then, despite his considerable score, his citation was short and sweet;

'A bold and skilful officer who has accounted for three enemy aeroplanes and two balloons during recent operations.'

By the time that was written in the autumn of 1918, Soden had more than 20 victories to his credit!

No 32 Sqn

Receiving its first SE 5as in the final weeks of 1917, No 32 Sqn had originally been formed in January 1916 at Netheravon, in Wiltshire, from a nucleus of personnel drawn from No 21 Sqn. Like most RFC scouting units of this period, it had been equipped with a series of

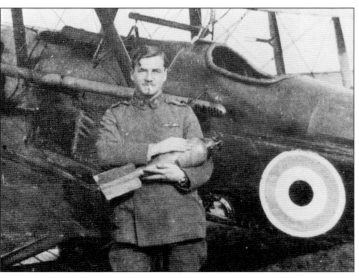

Australian Capt E J Stephens DFC was No 41 Sqn's fourth-ranking ace with 13 victories. He is seen here standing in front of SE 5a F5519 '1', which has had its headrest removed. Stephens, who claimed three victories with the aircraft in September-October 1918, is cradling a 20-lb Cooper bomb

Pilots of No 32 Sqn study a map on the fuselage of an SE 5a at Beauvois aerodrome, near St Pol, in May 1918. These young volunteers had come from America, Canada, New Zealand, England and South Africa. Lt C Hooper of the USAS is standing at the extreme right in this photograph *(Bruce Robertson)*

Capt W A Tyrell MC was No 32 Sqn's ranking ace with 17 victories, 12 of which he claimed in SE 5as. This aircraft – B8391 – with the number '3' on the top port wing, boasts an unusual camouflage scheme. Tyrell claimed none of his victories in this particular machine, although he was flying it when he was shot down by ground fire and killed on 9 June 1918

pusher types such as the FB 5 and DH 2 until the latter aircraft were replaced by back-staggered DH 5s in the early summer of 1917. The Airco scouts would remain on strength with No 32 Sqn at Droglandt until March 1918, these aircraft being flown alongside the ever-growing ranks of SE 5as.

The new Royal Aircraft Factory machines were warmly received by squadron pilots, who were keen to see the back of the DH 5s so that they could get away from the hazardous mission of ground strafing over the trenches. To a man, they were keen to take on German fighters in an aircraft that was more of a match for the Fokker Dr Is and Albatros D III/Vs that had been harassing them for the previous six months.

Just eight pilots from No 32 Sqn would achieve SE 5a acedom, with combat veteran Capt Walter A Tyrell MC leading the way with 12 victories. One of three soldier sons of Alderman Tyrell of Belfast, Walter was born in August 1898 and was living in Bangor, County Down, when war broke out in Europe. His first introduction to combat came upon joining the RNAS's Armoured Car Section in December 1914. By the time Tyrell transferred to the RFC in November 1915, he was a petty officer. Trained as a pilot, he joined No 32 Sqn in the autumn of 1917, and succeeded in claiming five victories with the DH 5, despite its generally poor performance.

Between 7 April and 6 June 1918, Tyrell claimed a further 12 victories in SE 5a B8374, earning him the MC. However, on 9 June his luck ran out. Although No 32 Sqn now engaged German fighters far more frequently, the unit was still being called on to strafe German troops in support of Allied ground offensives. Conducting just such a mission, Tyrell's SE 5a seems to have been caught by ground fire from German trenches. It quickly rolled over at low altitude and dived straight into the ground. Despite having been in action for three-and-a-half years, Walter Tyrell was still two months short of his 20th birthday when he was killed. One of his brothers – John, aged 23 – also died in a flying accident that same month.

American Capt Alvin A Callender from New Orleans was No 32 Sqn's next highest scorer with the SE 5a. Having joined the RFC in Canada, he arrived at the unit's Beauvois base in May 1918. His

modest tally of eight victories – all bar one of these being Fokker D VIIs – belies his flying capabilities as a flight leader. He was shot down in combat with *Jasta* 2 on 30 October 1918, Callender being extricated from the wreckage of his SE 5a and rushed to a nearby Canadian field hospital, although he succumbed to his injuries two days later. Forty years on, in April 1958, Naval Air Station New Orleans was renamed Alvin Callender Field in honour of the fallen aviator.

Capt John O Donaldson DFC and Bar DSC(US) was the second of four Americans to 'make ace' flying SE 5as with No 32 Sqn. Hailing from Fort Yates, North Dakota, he had joined the USAS and been sent to the RAF unit to gain combat experience. He certainly got plenty of the latter, claiming seven victories and receiving the British DFC and Bar and the American DSC. However, on 1 September 1918, 15-victory ace Theodor Quandt of *Jasta* 36 ended Donaldson's budding career as a fighter pilot when he forced him down in German-held territory and the American was captured. He managed to escape the following day, but he was quickly apprehended. On 9 September, Donaldson's bid for freedom was more successful, and he managed to reach neutral Holland by the end of the month. Continuing to fly post-war, Donaldson was killed in a flying accident near Philadelphia on 7 September 1930, aged 33.

Capt Frank L 'Buddy' Hale DFC of Syracuse, New York, was another American ace to enjoy success with No 32 Sqn in the late summer of 1918, the 23-year-old downing seven Fokker D VIIs in just a matter of weeks. Prior to his service with the RFC, Hale had spent time in uniform with the 4th Cavalry, New York National Guard, in 1914-15, followed by the Ambulance Service on the Mexican border in 1916. Rejected by the US Signal Corps (US military aviation in those days was no more than a section of the Signal Corps), Hale joined the RFC instead, and was eventually posted to No 32 Sqn. He also saw service with No 85 Sqn in the final weeks of the war, and remained with this unit as part of the occupation force in Germany.

Hale joined the US Army Air Corps prior to America's entry into World War 2, and travelled back to the UK with the Eighth Air Force in 1943. However, a heart condition forced his retirement, and he gained employment with Bell Aircraft Corporation. He subsequently died two months before his 50th birthday on 7 June 1944.

Capt A A Callender was one of five Americans to 'make ace' with No 32 Sqn in 1918. The highest scorer of the group with eight victories, he succumbed to wounds he had sustained dogfighting with *Jasta* 2 on 30 October 1918

Capt John O Donaldson DFC and Bar DSC(US) destroyed seven Fokker D VIIs in 1918 whilst flying with No 32 Sqn. He was himself shot down and captured on 1 September, but escaped twice, the second time successfully. The ribbon on his left breast is the initial version of the DFC, which was later changed to the more familiar diagonal stripes

This is the No 32 Sqn B Flight SE 5a (E5939) that Capt J O Donaldson was shot down in by 15-victory ace Theodor Quandt of *Jasta* 36 on 1 September 1918. The American had claimed five victories with the aircraft prior to its demise

The final American ace in No 32 Sqn was 20-year-old Lt Bogart Rogers DFC from Los Angeles, who scored six victories. He left Stanford University and travelled to Canada in September 1917 to join the RFC, and by the early summer of 1918 he was flying SE 5as with No 32 Sqn. Rogers wrote home about his fifth victory on 27 September 1918;

'We were escorting bombers on an expedition to a Hun aerodrome. As usual, wind and sun were against us. Over the objective, seven Huns attacked the bombers, and we went down on them. I dived on one, who half-rolled away when I started shooting. I pulled out in a left-hand climbing turn, and right in front of me was a Hun in a stall, nose up almost vertically, with the machine scarcely moving. It was a lovely target, so I gave it to him with both guns. He slipped out, then burst into flames. It's a nasty sight even if it is a Hun, but you're sure you have them that way. About ten seconds later, (Lt G E B) Lawson got another in flames.

'I went down on another Hun who was after the bombers, scared him away, and then got below everyone. The whole squadron was going around and around, and more Huns came up, and being unable to get back into the scrap, I came home under the bombers.'

South African Lt G E B Lawson DFC, whom Rogers mentions in his letter, achieved six victories (five in E1399) with No 32 Sqn. He was killed as a passenger in a flight in November 1922. Rogers died in Burbank, California, in July 1966.

One of only two English-born pilots (the other was Capt W B Green DFC Ld'H, who scored seven victories) to achieve ace status in the SE 5a with No 32 Sqn, Capt Arthur Claydon DFC was actually living in Canada when war was declared. Originally from Lincolnshire, he had joined the Militia in Winnipeg at the age of 18, then progressed to the Canadian Field Artillery. Arriving in France in the autumn of 1917, Claydon claimed his first victory – a two-seater – on 20 November while flying the DH 5. He had added six more to his score, flying SE 5a C1089, by the time he was shot down and killed on 8 July by 31-victory ace Paul Billik of *Jasta* 2. The fallen ace's DFC was subsequently gazetted on 3 August 1918.

New Yorker Capt F L Hale DFC also achieved seven Fokker D VII victories with No 32 Sqn in 1918, scoring all of his successes in August-September in SE 5a E4026

Capt A Claydon DFC was another ace to score seven victories with No 32 Sqn, although his first came in November 1917 in a DH 5. He was himself shot down and killed by 31-victory ace Paul Billik of *Jasta* 52 on 8 July 1918. The letter 'A' on the forward fuselage denotes the flight to which this SE 5a was assigned, rather than serving as the individual aircraft letter. The latter marking only appeared on the uppersurface of the scout's top port wing

No 24 Sqn

The last unit to receive SE 5as in 1917 was No 24 Sqn, which will always be famous for becoming the RFC's first ever truly dedicated fighter (or scout) squadron when it was equipped with DH 2s in January 1916. Formed three months earlier in Hounslow, west London, from a nucleus of personnel drawn from No 17 Sqn, the unit had been sent into action from Bertangles in February 1916. No 24 Sqn's first permanent CO was Maj Lanoe Hawker VC DSO, who joined the unit in September 1915. He had earned lasting fame in the months

Maj T F Hazell DSO DFC and
Bar MC achieved 23 SE 5a victories
(including ten kite balloons) with
No 24 Sqn in 1918 to add to his
20 Nieuport Scout claims with
No 1 Sqn the previous year
(*T Mellor-Ellis*)

South African Capt H D Barton DFC
and Bar (left) scored 19 victories
with No 24 Sqn between 18
February and 2 October 1918
(*M O'Connor*)

prior to No 24 Sqn's formation when he became Britain's first ace. Hawker was also the first scout pilot to receive the VC. He failed to add to his seven victories during his 14 months as CO of No 24 Sqn, and eventually lost his life in a legendary dogfight with Manfred von Richthofen on 23 November 1916.

No 24 Sqn held on to its obsolescent DH 2s until June 1917, when the unit re-equipped with DH 5s at Flez. Following six months of service with the Airco fighter, No 24 Sqn finally began to receive SE 5as from 17 December 1917.

By war's end, No 24 Sqn had produced more than 30 aces, placing it on a par with No 56 Sqn in respect to the number of successful pilots to have served with the unit. Some 19 of these aces had scored five or more victories with the SE 5a.

No 24 Sqn's ranking ace was Maj Tom Falcon Hazell DSO MC DFC and Bar, who arrived at No 24 Sqn as a flight commander in June 1918 with 20 victories already to his credit. Born in Galway in August 1892, Hazell had joined the Southern Irish Horse in September 1914 and been commissioned the following month in the 7th Battalion, Royal Inniskilling Fusiliers. Serving in France until 1916, Hazell had then transferred to the RFC. Joining No 1 Sqn at the end of that year, he would enjoy great success in Nieuport 17/23/24/27 Scouts between March and August 1917 (see *Osprey Aircraft of the Aces 33 – Nieuport Aces of World War 1* for further details). Indeed, his tally of 20 victories brought him both the MC and promotion to flight commander .

Returning to England for a well earned rest, Hazell spent time as an instructor at the Central Flying School until posted to No 24 Sqn at Conteville in June 1918 to serve as the unit's A Flight commander. The SE 5a allowed Hazell to make the most of his vast combat experience, and he had claimed a further 23 victories (including ten kite balloons) by October – nine of these were scored in E1388. That same month he was given command of Camel-equipped No 203 Sqn, but he failed to add to his tally of 43 victories. Remaining in the RAF post-war, Hazell commanded Nos 45, 55, 111 and 60 Sqns, and died in Ireland in 1946.

Capt Horace D Barton DFC and Bar was No 24 Sqn's second most successful SE 5a ace, with 19 victories to his credit. Born in South Africa in November 1891, he had seen two years of service in German Southwest and East Africa in 1914-16, prior to travelling to England and joining the RFC. Once trained as a pilot, Barton was posted to SE 5a-equipped No 84 Sqn in November 1917 and then sent to No 24 Sqn two months later. Amongst his victories were two German aircraft brought down behind British lines. One was a DFW two-seater (26 July 1918) and the other a Fokker D VII (17 June 1918) flown by 27-victory ace Kurt Wüsthoff of *Jasta* 15 – the latter success was shared with

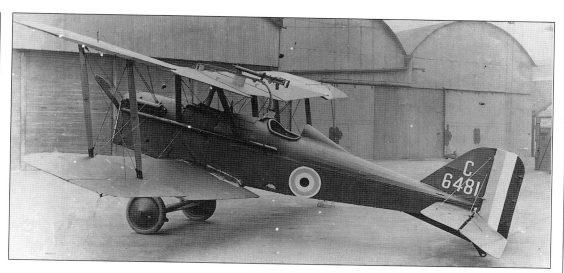

SE 5a C6481 was photographed soon after it was rolled out of the Royal Aircraft Factory plant at Farnborough in the spring of 1918. Issued to No 24 Sqn, the aircraft was used by Capt H D Barton to claim seven of his victories (including a solitary kite balloon) between 6 June and 4 August 1918 (*Bruce/Leslie*)

fellow No 24 Sqn aces Capts I D R McDonald MC DFC and G O Johnson MC CdG, as well as Lt C E Walton.

Wüsthoff was the second German ace to fall to Barton, for he had downed Hans Joachim Wolff (ten victories, including Lt J A McCudden) of *Jasta* 11 on 16 May 1918. Horace Barton saw further service in World War 2 as an intelligence officer in the South African Air Force (SAAF).

Fellow No 24 Sqn ace Capt I D R McDonald MC DFC claimed 17 victories with the SE 5a, as well as three with the DH 5. Born in Antigua, in the British West Indies, in September 1898, little is known about his military service prior to joining No 24 Sqn in late 1917. McDonald quickly announced his arrival in the frontline with three victories in the DH 5 in November and December. He 'made ace' with the destruction of two Fokker Dr Is on 26 February 1918, and by the time he claimed his final victory (Kurt Wüsthoff's Fokker D VII) on 17 June, his score stood at 20. McDonald was then rested, and left the RAF in early 1919.

He rejoined again the following year, and was serving in Mesopotamia when his aircraft was shot down by ground fire near Dangatora on 21 September 1921. He was summarily executed by local tribesmen shortly afterwards.

No 24 Sqn's fourth-ranking ace was 19-year-old Australian Capt Andrew K Cowper MC and two Bars, and he too scored 17 victories with the SE 5a. Although born in Bingara, New South Wales, in November 1898, he was educated at Eastbourne College in Sussex, and joined the Royal Sussex Regiment after completing his studies in 1916. Switching to the RFC in May 1917, Cowper joined No 24 Sqn in August 1917 and claimed two Albatros D IIIs destroyed whilst flying the DH 5, prior to the unit switching to the SE 5a. He had 'made ace' on 19 February 1918, and by 29 March was a flight commander with 19 victories to his credit.

Cowper also flew 20 ground-attack sorties during the last ten days of March, receiving two Bars to his MC for these daring, and dangerous, attacks. The citation that accompanied the second Bar read as follows;

'He bombed enemy troops who were entrenching, and caused great havoc and confusion. He made repeated and determined attacks, in spite of heavy hostile fire, and eventually forced the enemy to retire from their

Little known ace Capt I D R McDonald MC DFC was No 24 Sqn's second-highest scorer with 20 victories (17 in SE 5as) (*Bruce Robertson*)

Lt T M Harries of No 24 Sqn claimed his fifth SE 5a victory and (11th overall) in this machine – F5459 'Y' – on 29 October 1918. The aircraft was being tested with low wing dihedral when this photograph was taken in the final weeks of the war (*L A Rogers*)

trench. He returned to his aerodrome for more bombs and ammunition, and, going out a second time, attacked enemy troops and transport and threw them into confusion. He went out on two other occasions on the same day with equal success. Later, while cooperating with an infantry attack, he obtained four direct hits with bombs on an encampment, and forced several parties of the enemy to retire from their frontline. He showed magnificent dash and determination.'

Exhausted following his efforts over the previous eight weeks, Cowper was posted back to England for a rest in April. He later served in Germany (with No 79 Sqn, equipped with Sopwith Dolphins) and India straight after the war, before retiring from the RAF on 13 February 1920 and returning home. A successful horticulturalist, Andrew Cowper served again in World War 2 with the Royal Australian Air Force (RAAF), and eventually passed away in Australia in June 1980.

Like No 32 Sqn, No 24 Sqn also had a small contingent of American pilots within its ranks in 1918, and the most successful of these was Capt W C 'Bill' Lambert DFC. Born in Irontown, Ohio, in August 1894, he had made his first flight (as a passenger) in a Wright biplane on 4 July 1910. Working in Canada when World War 1 started, Lambert enlisted in the RFC in 1915, and by March 1918 he had joined No 24 Sqn. Although his final score is unclear, his official tally was 18 victories (including two balloons) between April and August. A flight commander by the time he was invalided back to the UK suffering from combat fatigue, he became a successful businessman post-war. Serving with the USAAF in World War 2, he rose to the rank of lieutenant colonel in the US Air Force (USAF) Reserve.

Bill Lambert wrote two books about his flying experiences, and I reviewed his volume *Combat Report* in 1973. I found it both evocative and interesting, and in my review I quoted the following paragraph;

'I notice one D VII at the edge of the scrap by himself. Back on the stick, full throttle and I start to climb and circle in behind the Fokker, who is watching the fighting near him. He has not seen me, and I slip into a good spot 50 yards behind. My eye is fixed to the Aldis (sight), my right thumb on the gun button and the throttle between the fingers of my left hand. I move in close. He is a perfect picture in my sights as I press for both guns. The pilot jerks in his seat, turns and looks back at me, his eyes staring in disbelief. The aeroplane falls off into a spin.'

Bill thanked me for my review, and also pointed out in his letter that his score, according to the curator of the USAF Museum at Wright-Patterson Air Force Base, was 19$\frac{1}{2}$ aircraft and two balloons destroyed. This information had come from the Air Ministry in London. Bill Lambert died in his native Irontown, Ohio, where he had worked all his life, in March 1982.

High-scoring Irish pilot Capt George McElroy MC and two Bars DFC appears next in No 24 Sqn's list of aces, with 16 of his 47 victories being claimed with the unit. As his biographical notes at the beginning of this chapter reveal, he achieved these successes in between two spells with No 40 Sqn.

In contrast to the well documented career of Capt McElroy, little is known about 15-victory ace Lt Herbert B Richardson MC DFC. Although born in Kent in May 1898, he was living in Oxford in 1914 when war broke out, so he joined the Oxford and Bucks Light Infantry. Richardson served only briefly in France before transferring to the RFC, and his victories were all scored between February and April 1918. These included three Pfalz Scouts in one action on 21 March in his favoured SE 5a D279 – he claimed his last seven victories with this aircraft. Post-war, Richardson found employment in civil aviation circles, and he was killed near Madrid on 14 February 1922 when the aeroplane he was flying in as a passenger crashed during a demonstration flight.

The last No 24 Sqn ace to achieve a score in double figures with the SE 5a was Lt Ronald T Mark MC and Bar. Born in Newcastle-on-Tyne in 1898, again there are few details pertaining to Mark's early war career prior to his joining No 24 Sqn in early 1918. He claimed 14 victories between 18 February and 3 May 1918, and arguably his most memorable sortie took place on 21 May. Mark received the Bar to his MC for his bravery on this mission, the citation for the award reading as follows;

'This officer and another pilot (seven-victory ace Capt C N Lowe MC DFC) were escorting a formation of machines engaged on bombing a village, when seven enemy scouts attacked the bombers. They both attacked these scouts, but at the outset the other pilot's machine was set on fire, and 2Lt Mark's right-hand top plane broke. During the fight that ensued each came to the rescue of the other. 2Lt Mark first caused the other pilot's pursuer to break off his attack, and then the other pilot shot down the scout attacking 2Lt Mark. The action of these officers, in practically immanoeuvrable machines, in coming to the rescue of each other in turn showed courage and self-sacrifice of a very high order.'

Upon landing, Mark's SE 5a burst into flames, but he managed to scramble clear without injury.

Another ace of note to serve with No 24 Sqn was Lt Herbert B Redler MC. A Somerset man, born in

American Capt William C Lambert DFC made his first flight in a Wright biplane as a passenger on 4 July 1910. He went on to join the RFC and fly SE 5as with No 24 Sqn, claiming 18 victories
(*E F Cheesman*)

SE 5a ace Capt C N Lowe MC claimed seven victories with No 24 Sqn in 1918, having previously been credited with two successes flying FE 2bs with No 11 Sqn the previous year. Lowe's final victory was achieved in this aircraft (E1293 '4') on 1 July 1918

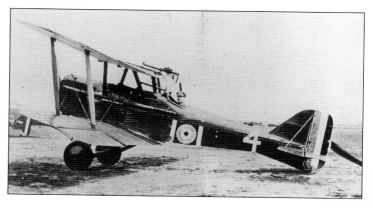

January 1897, he had scored three victories flying Nieuports with No 40 Sqn in 1917 prior to joining No 24 Sqn as a flight commander in March 1918. Redler's first victory with the SE 5a was the Fokker Dr I flown by 27-victory ace Adolf von Tutschek, commander of JG II. It seems that one of Redler's bullets creased the German's skull, forcing him to make a hurried landing. Although von Tutschek waved to his pilots as they circled him, he was later found dead alongside his machine.

Redler went on to claim six more victories with No 24 Sqn prior to returning to England on 21 April. Two months later, on 21 June, he was killed in a DH 9 crash near Tewkesbury, in Gloucestershire.

── No 2 Sqn, Australian Flying Corps ──

We end this chapter by introducing the only Australian-manned SE 5a unit in World War 1. No 2 Sqn, Australian Flying Corps (AFC), was originally formed at Kantara, in Egypt, in September 1916, but the unit was redesignated as No 68 Sqn by the RFC upon its arrival at Harlaxton, in Lincolnshire, in January 1917. The DH 5-equipped unit was sent to Baizieux in September 1917, and it had begun receiving SE 5as at this location in January 1918. The new fighter's arrival coincided with the unit being renumbered No 2 Sqn AFC.

Having seen plenty of action since their arrival in France (especially in support of the nearby Cambrai offensive of November 1917), the Australian pilots quickly completed their conversion onto the SE 5a, and once again took the fight to the enemy in their sector of the front.

Fourteen pilots claimed ace status in the SE 5a whilst serving with No 2 Sqn AFC, and leading the pack was Capt Francis R Smith DFC with 16 victories. Born in Brisbane in 1896, he had worked pre-war as a clerk prior to enlisting in the Australian Infantry. Serving with distinction in the 31st Battalion, Smith was awarded an MC in 1916. Transferring to

The pilots of No 2 Sqn AFC, and their mascots, pose for a photograph in 1918. Included in their number are the following aces – Capt G H Blaxland (back row, fifth from left), Capt A G Clark (front row, extreme left), Capt E D Cummings DFC (back row, second from left), Capt H G Forrest DFC (front row, third from left), Capt L H Holden MC (top row, extreme right – he claimed one DH 5 victory and four with the SE 5a), Capt R L Manuel DFC (centre row, extreme right), Capt R W McKenzie MC (centre row, fourth from left), Maj R C Phillipps MC and Bar DFC (front row, fifth from left) and Capt F R Smith DFC (front row, sixth from left) (*AWM*)

the AFC the following year, he joined No 2 Sqn AFC on 28 February 1918 and quickly found his feet in the SE 5a. Smith claimed his first victory on 9 May, and 'made ace' on 3 September. His favoured mount from early August was C6403, and he scored his last 13 victories in this aircraft – including four Fokker D VIIs in two separate actions on 14 October. These also proved to be his final successes.

Just 24 hours prior to the Armistice, Smith was shot down in C6403 by ground fire during a strafing sortie, but in the confusion of the battle front he evaded capture and made it back to Allied lines two days later.

The second-ranking ace in No 2 Sqn AFC was Maj Roy C Phillipps MC and Bar DFC, who claimed 15 victories, all but his first with the SE 5a – his initial success came while flying a DH 5 during the Battle of Cambrai in November 1917. Although born in North Sydney in March 1892, Phillipps was raised in Western Australia, and he was working as a practising accountant in Perth when war came. Like Francis Smith, he too enlisted in the Australian Infantry, seeing much action in France with the 28th Battalion. Promoted to captain and awarded the MC, Phillipps suffered a serious leg wound that left one of his limbs partially paralysed.

Such an injury should have seen Phillipps invalided home to Australia, but keen to keep fighting, he wangled a transfer to the AFC. Working as No 68 Sqn's adjutant, he eventually applied for pilot training in May 1917. Upon earning his 'wings', Phillipps was posted to No 32 Sqn in August to gain experience with the DH 5, and he was shot down by ground fire near Ypres whilst with the unit. Rejoining No 68 Sqn the following month, he flew countless strafing sorties in the DH 5 until the aircraft was replaced by the SE 5a in January 1918.

Serving as a flight commander throughout his time with the Australian unit, Phillipps' greatest day with No 2 Sqn AFC was on 12 June 1918, when he claimed four victories in a single patrol – one of his victims was the CO of *Jasta* 26, 12-victory ace Fritz Loerzer.

Phillipps achieved his 14 successes in just two SE 5as – C9541, in which he scored six victories, and D6860, with which he downed his last eight. Lt T J Hammond scored a victory in the former machine on 11 June 1918, but it was becoming 'war weary' by then and was soon taken off operations. D6860 was delivered to No 2 Sqn AFC at the end of May, and Lt L J Primrose claimed a victory with it on 1 June. Once Phillipps stopped using the fighter, the SE 5a was taken over by Lt E E Davies, who scored three more victories with it, making 12 in all. Davies had to crash-land D6860 on 18 October after being hit by ground fire.

Rested in August, Phillipps was promoted to major and placed in charge of No 6 Training Squadron. He became a farmer post-war, but joined the RAAF in World War 2 and was killed in a flying accident in May 1940 whilst serving as CO of No 2 Elementary Flying Training School at Archerfield, in Queensland.

Capts R C Phillipps MC and Bar DFC (left) and H G Forrest DFC of No 2 Sqn, AFC, were two of the four pilots to achieve double figure scores with the unit in France in 1918. Phillipps claimed 15 victories (14 with SE 5as and one with the DH 5) and Forrest got 11 (all with the SE 5a) (*T Mellor-Ellis*)

Capt R L Manuel DFC was the third-ranking ace of No 2 Sqn, AFC, claiming 12 victories with the SE 5a (*T Mellor-Ellis*)

SE 5a E5965 'X' of No 2 Sqn, AFC, was used by Lt G J Cox on 27 August 1918 to claim three of his five victories. He was subsequently shot down in this machine on 21 September when a stray artillery shell knocked the engine from its bearers, causing the fighter to spin down literally out of control and crash behind enemy lines. Cox was soon captured, and he spent the rest of the the war as a PoW (*L A Rogers*)

Scoring 12 victories with No 2 Sqn AFC, 22-year-old Capt Roby L Manuel DFC hailed from Kerang, in Victoria. A farmer pre-war, he also saw action in the Australian Infantry prior to flight training and then a posting to No 2 Sqn AFC in February 1918. Manuel claimed all of his successes between 2 April and 24 September, downing five aircraft in SE 5a B184 and seven in C1948. He was forced to switch aircraft after seven-victory Lt Frank Alberry made an emergency landing in B184 in late June when the scout's engine suffered oil pressure problems. The fighter was deemed NWR (not worth repairing), and Manuel duly switched to C1948. This latter machine was finally declared 'unfit for further service' in January 1919.

Manuel's 11th victim was Vzfw Kurt Brandt of *Jasta* 51, who crash-landed his Fokker D VII south of Droglandt on the morning of 16 September – his second success on this day. The German pilot had been badly wounded in the engagement, and Manuel landed alongside the fighter and tried to help Brandt. There was nothing he could do, however, and the pilot died a short while later – the Australian ace helped bury him.

Manuel also served his country again in World War 2 when he enlisted in the RAAF, and in the late 1960s he was still piloting his own light aeroplane. He died on 18 October 1975, just ten days after his 80th birthday.

Capt Gregory H Blaxland was one of the last pilots to achieve ace status with No 2 Sqn AFC, claiming his fifth victim on 14 October 1918. The grandson of the famous Australian explorer George Blaxland who, in 1813, had been a part of the first colonial expedition to cross the Blue Mountains in New South Wales, Gregory Blaxland was born in Broken Hill, New South Wales, in March 1896. When war came he was studying electrical engineering in Fremantle, Western Australia, and like many Australians from this state, he joined the 10th Australian Light Horse. Blaxland switched to the AFC in June 1917, however, and in February 1918 he was posted to No 2 Sqn AFC after completing his training.

He had claimed three victories by early May, and looked to be well on his way to 'making ace'. However, on the 4th of that month Blaxland accidentally shot down a French SPAD from SPA86, killing its pilot, Adjutant Renault. No 2 Sqn AFC failed in its attempts to cover up the

Capt E E Davies DFC of No 2 Sqn AFC, scored seven victories with the unit between 27 August and 4 November 1918 – he claimed a trio of successes on the latter date. Three of his victims were Fokker D VIIs, but not this particular aircraft (*T Mellor-Ellis*)

Capt R W McKenzie MC scored his fifth and sixth victories in SE 5a C5382 'Z' of No 2 Sqn, AFC, on 22 and 23 March 1918. Note the fighter's distinctive boomerang marking aft of its identification letter (*L A Rogers*)

incident and Blaxland was posted back to England, and No 8 Training Squadron AFC, where he was injured in a flying accident on 1 July. Fully recovered by late September, he rejoined No 2 Sqn AFC and quickly made up for lost time by downing five Fokker D VIIs between 4 October and 4 November. Although made a flight commander, Blaxland was never decorated almost certainly because of the friendly fire incident. Living in Sydney post-war, he eventually passed away in August 1969.

Seven-victory ace Capt Richard W Howard MC has the unenviable distinction of being the only No 2 Sqn AFC ace to be killed in action. Born in Sydney in October 1896 and raised in Newcastle, New South Wales, he was studying engineering in nearby Hamilton when war came. Joining the Australian Army engineers in September 1915, Howard served in France from March to December 1916, when transferred to the AFC. Assigned as a pilot to No 68 Sqn in early April 1917, he was then briefly posted to DH 4-equipped No 57 Sqn the following month, before returning to the Australian-manned unit in July.

Howard claimed his first victory flying DH 5s during the Cambrai offensives in November 1917, but he was also forced down three times during this period whilst participating in strafing missions. He had been made a flight commander by the time No 2 Sqn AFC was issued with SE 5as, and flying D212, he claimed seven victories between 28 February and 18 March. However, four days after scoring his final success, Howard was shot down near Vermond in D212 by Ltn Hans Böhning of *Jasta* 79 – the Australian survived the engagement, but subsequently succumbed to his wounds. Howard was Böhning's sixth victim, and the German would eventually score a total of 17 kills.

NEW SQUADRONS IN 1918

By the start of the final year of the war, the SE 5a had become firmly established in the RFC's fighter force. It, together with Sopwith's F1 Camel, were the two main British fighters, the Camel generally operating at lower altitudes – where it also performed ground attack sorties – while the SE 5a remained at medium to high altitude, either escorting bombers or providing top cover for the Camels below. SE 5a units also routinely attacked ground targets too, although the Camel seemed more adept at this dangerous task. Undoubtedly, the pilot's more forward position in the Sopwith fighter meant that they had a better view of the ground, thus allowing them to react quicker to any sudden obstructions that might appear ahead of them.

The only other British single-seat fighter to see regular combat on the Western Front for much of 1918 was the Sopwith Dolphin. Four squadrons of this type arrived during the Spring of 1918, and it was not until the final weeks of the war that the Camel's planned replacement – the Sopwith Snipe – arrived to re-equip just two units prior to the Armistice (see *Osprey Aircraft of the Aces 48 – Dolphin and Snipe Aces of World War 1* for further details).

This well-known photograph of No 1 Sqn, taken at Clairmarais South on 3 July 1918, not only shows American aces 1Lt Duerson Knight (standing in the front row at far left) and Capt Howard Kullberg too (in the cockpit of C1835 in the foreground), but also Knight's SE 5a (C1106 'Y') in which he made three claims. Kullberg also achieved two victories in B8254

Appropriately, the first of three RFC units to make the switch to SE 5as in the new year was No 1 Sqn. Embroiled in the conflict in France since March 1915, it had flown a variety of aeroplane types in the early days before re-equipping with Morane scouts, which were in turn replaced by a sequence of Nieuport fighters – the unit also operated a handful of two-seaters from the same manufacturer. Indeed, it was one of the last Nieuport-equipped squadrons in the RFC to convert to the SE 5a. The first examples of the latter aircraft started to arrive at No 1 Sqn's long term base at the Asylum Ground, in Bailleul, on 18 January.

The squadron had boasted the RFC's leading Nieuport ace in Capt Philip Fullard DSO MC and Bar, who had claimed 40 victories by the time he foolishly broke his leg playing football on 17 November 1917! Sent back to England to convalesce, his injury was so serious that he did not return to France, and so missed out on flying the SE 5a.

The title of top-scoring SE 5a ace in No 1 Sqn therefore went to Capt Percy Jack Clayson MC DFC, who was born in Croydon, Surrey, in June 1896. Jack – or 'Pip' as he was generally known – had joined the RNAS at the start of the war, and seen action with the 'senior service' in France from December 1914 until he transferred to the RFC in the summer of 1917. Clayson joined No 1 Sqn a month before Fullard suffered his accident, but did not score his first victory until 16 February 1918. He 'made ace' on 27 March, and was promoted to flight commander two months later. Clayson enjoyed great success during the May-July period, when he downed 21 aircraft and a solitary kite balloon. These successes took his final tally to 29 victories – ten more than No 1 Sqn's second-ranking SE 5a ace, Capt Howard A Kullberg DFC.

Included in this tally was a solitary Fokker Dr I from *Jasta* 14 on 9 June, which Clayson forced down behind British lines with the help of several SE 5a pilots from No 29 Sqn – the triplane's pilot, Gefr Reinhold Preiss, was taken prisoner. He had been flying *Staffelführer* Hans Werner's Dr I (583/17) at the time of his demise. Eight days earlier, on 1 June, seven-victory ace Werner had shot down No 40 Sqn CO, and SE 5a ace, Maj Roderic Dallas in this very triplane. The Dr I had since been relegated to Priess' use following Werner's receipt of a brand new Fokker D VII.

Clayson flew a variety of SE 5as, with 18 of his claims being made in C1114 'N', but by mid-August 1918 it was so worn out that it had to be scrapped. The ace had by then been posted back to Home Establishment in the UK. Clayson remained in the RAF post-war, serving with Nos 6 and 70 Sqns during the 1920s.

Capt Howard A Kullberg DFC was one of three American aces to serve with No 1 Sqn. Born in Somerville, Massachusetts, in September 1896, he had joined the RFC in Toronto in August 1917 after having been deemed too short to serve in the USAS. Sent to No 1 Sqn in May 1918 he had claimed four victories by the end of the month. All of these successes were shared with other pilots in the unit, as the British scoring system allowed for victories to be divided up when more then one aviator had taken part in the downing of a German machine. No 1 Sqn, in particular, seemed to like sharing out the laurels, with as many as six pilots being given credit for a single victory, thus boosting individual scores.

Ten of Kullberg's victories were shared (almost half of Clayson's were too), and being a flight commander, most of them were divided up

No 1 Sqn's top-scoring SE 5a pilot was Capt Percy 'Pip' Clayson MC DFC with 29 victories

Capt Howard Kullberg ended the war as No 1 Sqn second-ranking SE 5a ace with 19 victories to his credit. He had only joined the RFC after been rejected by the USAS for being too short! Kullberg received the DFC just prior to being badly wounded on 16 September 1918 (*E F Cheesman*)

between him and his men. He had increased his tally to 19 victories by 16 September, but minutes after downing a Fokker D VII near Valenciennes during a mid-morning patrol, he was hit three times in the leg by rounds fired by one of five German scouts that chased him back across the frontline. Kullberg saw out the remaining months of the war in hospital, before being sent home.

Unlike his high-scoring countryman, 25-year-old 1Lt Duerson Knight from Chicago, Illinois, had no problem enlisting in the USAS. Upon his arrival in the UK, he was attached to No 1 Sqn in May 1918 so as to gain combat experience. Knight remained with the unit until mid September, and in that time he was credited with ten victories. Eight of these were shared with other pilots (Kullberg received a shared credit in six of Knight's victories, for example), including a tenth of a kill for a Pfalz D III destroyed on 1 June and a similar share in the well-documented *Jasta* 14 Fokker Dr I captured on 9 June!

1Lt Duerson 'Dewey' Knight from Chicago gained ten victories with No 1 Sqn flying SE 5as in 1918. The last of these was a Fokker Dr I from *Jasta* 14 brought down behind Allied lines by a number of squadron pilots on 9 June

Transferred to the USAS in September, Knight failed to see any further combat prior to Armistice Day. He passed away in California in June 1983, aged 90.

The third American pilot to become an ace with No 1 Sqn was 23-year-old New Yorker Lt Francis Peabody Magoun MC. A Harvard graduate, he had offered his services to the Allied cause prior to America entering the war by joining the US Ambulance Service. Seeing action in France in 1916, he then returned home for a short while, prior to joining the RFC in the UK. Posted to No 1 Sqn in mid November 1917 while it was still flying Nieuports, Magoun did not score his first victory until 28 February 1918, by which time his unit was flying the SE 5a.

Harvard graduate Lt Francis Peabody Magoun MC, was yet another American to fly SE 5as and become an ace with No 1 Sqn. After the war he returned to academic life (*E F Cheesman*)

Having scored 27 SE 5/5a victories with No 56 Sqn in 1917, Capt R T C Hoidge MC and Bar returned to France in late 1918 and claimed his 28th success in this SE 5a with No 1 Sqn on 29 October (*Bruce/Leslie*)

Having increased his tally to four victories by 28 March, Magoun was then wounded on 10 April while strafing German troops. He was hospitalised until October, when he at last rejoined No 1 Sqn. Magoun finally scored his all important fifth victory on 28 October, and his unit claimed its final aerial successes of World War 1 just 24 hours later.

Remaining in England post-war, Magoun graduated from Cambridge University prior to returning to the United States. He later became an English professor at Harvard, specialising in Finnish studies. He died in June 1979.

Of the 14 pilots to score five or more kills with the SE 5a whilst serving with No 1 Sqn, only Capt Cecil C Clark had made previous claims with the Nieuport prior to the unit's re-equipment. Born in Norwich in 1898, and a veteran of combat in France with the Royal Field Artillery, Clark had joined the RFC in 1916 and been posted to No 1 Sqn in February of the following year. Claiming three victories with the Nieuport 17 in March 1917, he was hospitalised for an extended period of time the following month, and eventually returned to No 1 Sqn as C Flight Commander in April 1918. Seemingly making up for lost time, Clark claimed six aircraft and a kite balloon in just 16 days. Such a frenetic run of success could not last, however, and on 8 May (just 24 hours after scoring his final victory) he was shot down over German-held territory by six-victory ace Harry von Bülow-Bothkamp of *Jasta* 36 – Clark spent the rest of the war as a PoW.

Remaining in the RAF post-war, Clark had risen to the rank of squadron leader by 1939, but he died of natural causes that November.

No 1 Sqn aces Lt J C Bateman (seven victories), Capt H J Hamilton MC (six victories, three with the SE 5a) and Lt E E Owen (five victories) (*T Mellor-Ellis*)

No 64 SQN

Issued with SE 5as at virtually the same time as No 1 Sqn, No 64 Sqn was yet another of those units keen to retire its DH 5s and break free of the ground attack mission that had been its lot since its arrival at Le Hameau, due west of Arras, in October 1917. Formed at Sedgeford, on the north Norfolk coast, in August 1916 from a nucleus of personnel drawn from No 45 Sqn, the unit had flown F 20s, BE 2cs, FE 2bs and Pups prior to being sent to France with DH 5s under the command of Maj B E Smythies.

The unit had suffered high casualties whilst performing its low-level bombing/strafing missions during the Battle of Cambrai in November 1917, so news that SE 5as would soon be arriving at Le Hameau was greeted with great enthusiasm. It took some while for its pilots to convert not only to the new machine, but also to their new fighter role, so No 64 Sqn did not begin operations with the SE 5a until early March.

Capt J A Slater MC and Bar DFC was No 64 Sqn's leading ace with 22 victories, 21 of which were claimed with the SE 5a – his first success with the unit came in a DH 5. Slater also scored two victories in Nieuport Scouts with No 1 Sqn prior to joining No 64 Sqn

Californian Lt C A Bissonette shot down six German aircraft in the spring of 1918 flying SE 5as with No 64 Sqn. He also later served with No 24 Sqn, but claimed no victories with this unit (*E F Cheesman*)

The unit had claimed just two aerial victories in several months of frontline flying with the DH 5, and both of these had been claimed by No 64 Sqn's flight commanders, Capts J E Slater MC and Bar DFC and E R Tempest MC DFC. They would also go on to top the unit's 11-strong list of aces, and, on 8 March, it was them who downed the first of the many SE 5a victories to fall to No 64 Sqn – two other pilots also put in claims, one being future 11-victory ace Capt Tommy Rose DFC.

Born in November 1896, Jimmy Slater had served as a private with the Royal Sussex Regiment in France, before joining the Irish Rifles. Transferring to the RFC in 1915, he was posted as an observer to FB 5-equipped No 18 Sqn just as the unit deployed to France in November of that year. Slater undertook flying training 12 months later, and initially served with No 1 Sqn. He claimed his first two victories flying Nieuport 17s with this unit in February-March 1917, and then scored his third in a No 64 Sqn DH 5 on 30 November that same year.

With the arrival of the SE 5a in early 1918, Slater really hit his straps, 'making ace' on 11 March – just three days after claiming No 64 Sqn's first victory with the SE 5a. Indeed, March 1918 proved to be a particularly productive time for the veteran Slater, as there was no shortage of targets for him to engage thanks to the German offensive in Picardy, which began on the 21st. By month end, Slater had claimed ten victories (at least seven of them in SE 5a B147), with three of these coming on the opening day of the offensive. Three more followed in April and then, during May, he claimed eight victories in just 25 combats.

By the time Slater's tour ended in July and he was posted back to the Home Establishment in the UK, his score stood at 24 victories overall, with 21 of these being claimed with the SE 5a. He spent the rest of the war instructing, and remained in the RAF post-war. Slater served both at home and in the Middle East in the early 1920s, enjoying tours with Nos 20, 216 and, again, No 1 Sqn. In 1925 he moved to No 3 Sqn, before becoming an instructor at the Central Flying School. Slater was killed in a flying accident whilst still serving with this unit on 26 November 1925, just 24 hours short of his 29th birthday.

His son Robin also served in the RAF as a Halifax pilot in World War 2, during which time he won the DFC and AFC. Rising to the rank of wing commander, he told me two interesting stories about his father's flying escapades post-World War 1;

'After the war, my father went to RAF Sedgeford (No 3 Fighting School), where one of his delights was to fly through one end of a hangar and out the other side. One day, he was asked to put on a solo aerobatic display for Queen Alexandra, who had come over from Sandringham. It was not long, apparently, before the Queen turned to the CO of the base and said, "Order that young man down before he kills himself".

'Another favourite sport he had was to beat up the town of Hunstanton at chimney pot height at 8 o'clock on Saturday mornings. He visited each of his girlfriends' houses in turn. Surprisingly enough, the local authorities thought all this was quite in order. He was killed as a flying instructor at CFS, Upavon. It was the old story of an instructor not taking over control in time. Even so, he very nearly retrieved the situation. I often feel that with his terrific spirit and flair for the unorthodox, he would have reached high rank during World War 2, if only he had lived.'

Capt Edmund Roger Tempest MC DFC served alongside Jimmy Slater in No 64 Sqn in 1917-18. Born in Pontefract, West Yorkshire, in October 1894, he and his brother Wulston (who gained fame in the RFC for shooting down the Zeppelin L 31 on 1 October 1916) went to Canada as young men to become farmers in Saskatchewan. Both returned to join the King's Own Yorkshire Light Infantry in 1914, however, and then transferred to the RFC in early 1916.

Initially flying BE 2s with Nos 6 and 15 Sqns, Tempest became a fighter pilot when he was posted to No 64 Sqn in July 1917. Like Slater, he too claimed his solitary DH 5 victory on 30 November 1917, and he went on to destroy 16 aircraft between 8 March and 14 August 1918 (seven of the latter were downed by him in B74). Remaining in the RAF post-war, Capt Tempest died in 1921 whilst serving in Mesopotamia.

One of two No 64 Sqn pilots to claim 11 victories with the SE 5a, Capt Tommy Rose DFC flew with Tempest on many occasions in 1918. We corresponded during the 1960s, and he told me;

'Edmund Tempest was the brother of Wulston, who got the Potter's Bar "Zepp". Edmund was the greatest patrol leader I have ever known. I was in his flight initially, and I am certain that if the opportunities had come his way he would have been known as one of the greatest. Jimmy Slater was the opposite type. If an "archie" burst was close enough, he would loop round it. If one of his flight habitually left the patrol with "engine trouble", he would follow him down firing both guns!'

Born in Chilbolton, Hampshire, in January 1895, Rose joined the RFC in 1917 and was sent to No 64 Sqn in time to see action during the Battle of Cambrai. After his first victory claim on 8 March 1918, he downed his 11th, and last, aircraft on 14 August.

Rose remained in the RAF until 1927, serving for a time with No 43 Sqn. He then became Sales Manager with Phillips & Powis Aircraft Co Ltd in Reading, as well as being Chief Flying Instructor for the Northamptonshire Aero Club. Rose later found employment as pilot with the Anglo-American Oil Company. He also took part in many air races in the 1930s, winning the King's Cup Air Race in 1935 and participating in the race to Johannesburg that same year. In 1936 Rose used a Miles Falcon to establish a new record for the quickest flight to South Africa. He later became Chief Test pilot for the Miles Company. Post-World War 2, Rose managed Universal Flying Services, and he finally retired to the Channel Islands in the 1960s. He died in June 1968.

The second No 64 Sqn ace to claim 11 victories was 23-year-old Capt Phillip S Burge MC of Potter's Bar, Middlesex. A student at Marlborough College pre-war, he served with the Army early in the war and won the MM in the summer of 1916. Commissioned into the RFC the following year, Burge joined No 64 in October 1917 and later became a flight commander. His 11 victories were scored between 23 March and 22 July, but two days after this last claim he was shot down in flames over Seclin, probably by Marat Schumm of *Jasta* 52.

No 64 Sqn's second-ranking ace, Capt E R Tempest MC DFC claimed 17 victories with the unit, 16 of which were achieved in SE 5as

Capt Tommy Rose DFC was one of five aces to post a double figure score flying SE 5as with No 64 Sqn in 1918. He is seen here in the late 1930s, by which time Rose had become a successful air racer and test pilot

NO 74 SQN

The most successful of the new units to receive the SE 5a in terms of the number of aces it produced (17), No 74 Sqn had formed at Northolt, in Middlesex, in July 1917. Staffed with a nucleus of personnel drawn from

No 2 Training School, the unit performed training duties from London Colney until issued with SE 5as in March 1918 and sent to France.

No 74 Sqn was led into action from Clairmarais North by Maj Keith Caldwell, who already had nine victories to his credit from a previous tour with No 40 Sqn. Eight of these had come in Nieuport Scouts and the ninth in an SE 5a, prior to him being sent to England for a rest. He would enjoy even more success with No 74 Sqn, as detailed later in this chapter.

No 74 Sqn quickly gained a reputation for getting 'stuck in' primarily due to the exploits of its senior flight commander, Capt Edward 'Mick' Mannock VC DSO and Bar MC. He joined the unit with his score standing at 16 victories following his tour with No 40 Sqn the previous year – 15 of these successes were claimed in Nieuport Scouts, and just one, on 1 January 1918, in an SE 5a. Mannock's biographical details appear later in this chapter.

Although Mannock would claim 36 victories with No 74 Sqn, he would not top the list of aces in the unit. He was beaten into second place by Capt J I T Jones MM DSO MC DFC and Bar, who claimed 36 aircraft and a solitary kite balloon destroyed between 8 May and 7 August 1918.

Born in April 1896, James Ira Thomas Jones was a Welshman from St Clears, in Carmarthen, so inevitably he was known as 'Taffy'. Small in stature, but with a big heart and even bigger desire to defeat the Germans, he had joined the Territorial Army in 1913. Upon the outbreak of war, Jones had transferred to the RFC and became a lowly airman wireless operator. Soon he was in France with No 10 Sqn, flying occasionally as an observer in its BE 2cs. It was, however, whilst on the ground with a forward wireless receiving station that he gained the first of his decorations. In May 1916 a nearby gun battery came under fire from the German side of the lines and Jones duly rescued two wounded gunners, for which he received the MM and the rare Russian Medal of St George.

In October 1916 Jones formally became an observer with No 10 Sqn, and in May 1917 he returned to England to be commissioned as an officer and to train as a pilot. Once he had earned his wings, Jones was posted to No 74 Sqn while the new unit was still working up. He was assigned to Mannock's flight, and the ace soon became Jones' mentor.

Travelling to France with the unit in late March 1918, he claimed his first victory on 8 May, and by the end of that month his score stood at 15. Jones claimed seven more aircraft in June, nine in July and a further six in early August, taking his score to 37, with perhaps two more unconfirmed. By then he wore the ribbons of the MC, DFC and Bar and finally the DSO next to his MM, making made him the squadron's most decorated pilot. Fifteen of Jones' victories were scored in C1117, 13 in D6895 and another six in D6958.

One of Jones' first encounters (in C1117) was with a German Albatros C type two-seater on 18 May 1918. His victory on this date gave him ace status, and he recalled the engagement in a newspaper article in 1936;

'I met my adversary – a two-seater Albatros – at 17,000 ft over Zillebeke Lake, just east of Ypres, as he was returning from a reconnaissance flight over our lines. I was well below him, and I sneaked up under his tail, hoping to catch him unawares. The German observer, however, was on the alert, and when I was about 400 yards away he opened fire. I waited until I got to within (*text continues on page 64*)

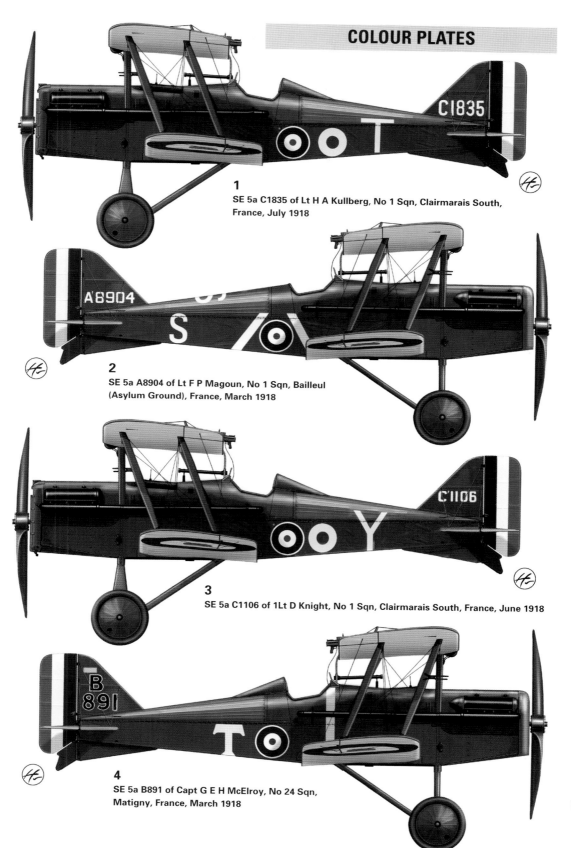

1
SE 5a C1835 of Lt H A Kullberg, No 1 Sqn, Clairmarais South,
France, July 1918

2
SE 5a A8904 of Lt F P Magoun, No 1 Sqn, Bailleul
(Asylum Ground), France, March 1918

3
SE 5a C1106 of 1Lt D Knight, No 1 Sqn, Clairmarais South, France, June 1918

4
SE 5a B891 of Capt G E H McElroy, No 24 Sqn,
Matigny, France, March 1918

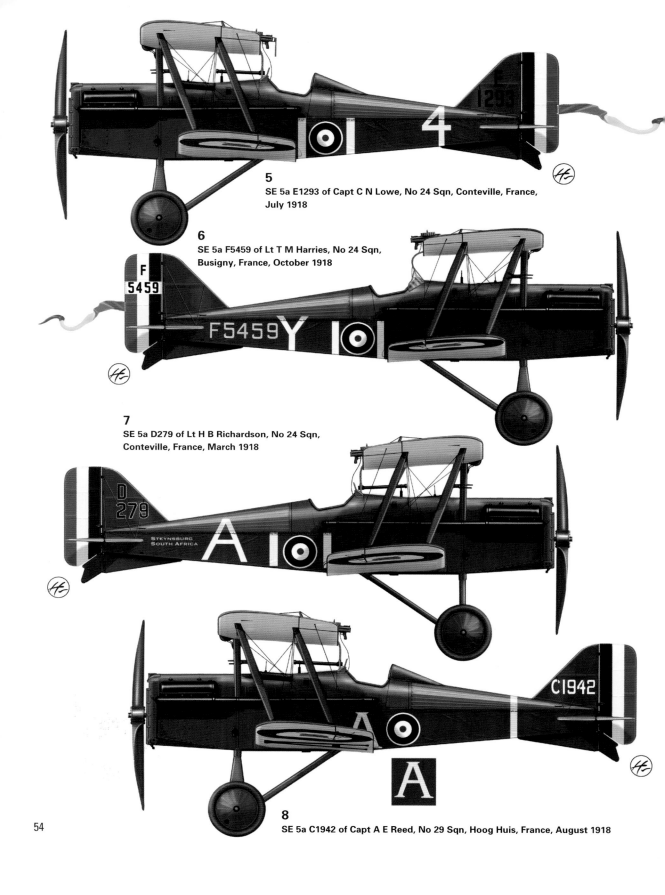

5
SE 5a E1293 of Capt C N Lowe, No 24 Sqn, Conteville, France, July 1918

6
SE 5a F5459 of Lt T M Harries, No 24 Sqn, Busigny, France, October 1918

7
SE 5a D279 of Lt H B Richardson, No 24 Sqn, Conteville, France, March 1918

STEYNSBURG
SOUTH AFRICA

8
SE 5a C1942 of Capt A E Reed, No 29 Sqn, Hoog Huis, France, August 1918

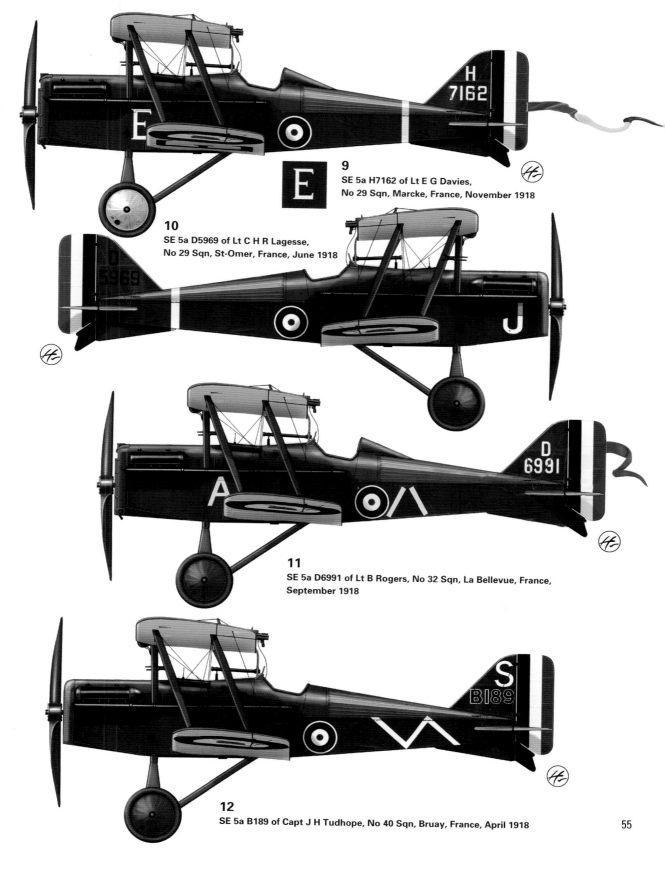

9
SE 5a H7162 of Lt E G Davies,
No 29 Sqn, Marcke, France, November 1918

10
SE 5a D5969 of Lt C H R Lagesse,
No 29 Sqn, St-Omer, France, June 1918

11
SE 5a D6991 of Lt B Rogers, No 32 Sqn, La Bellevue, France,
September 1918

12
SE 5a B189 of Capt J H Tudhope, No 40 Sqn, Bruay, France, April 1918

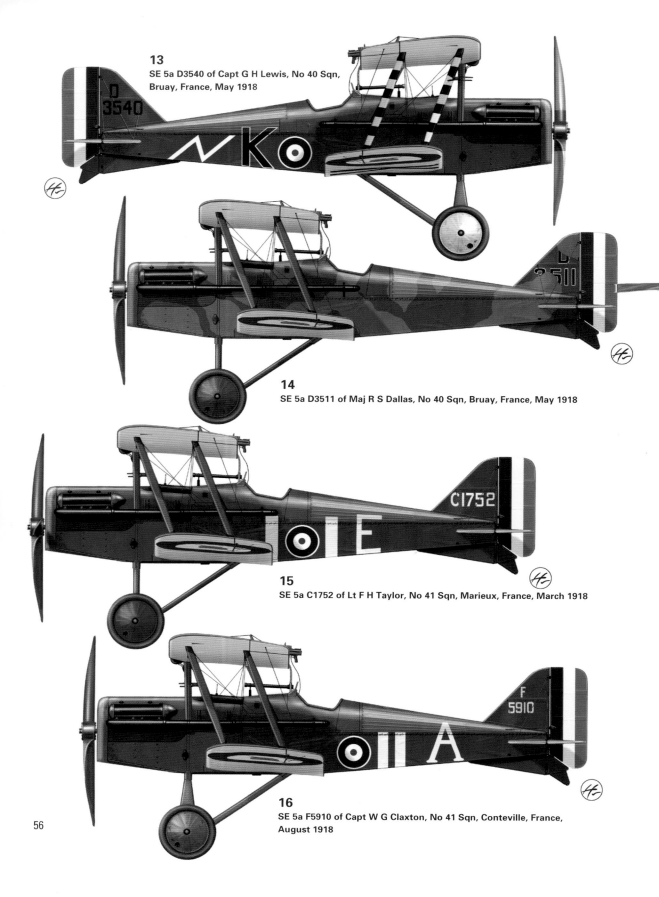

13
SE 5a D3540 of Capt G H Lewis, No 40 Sqn,
Bruay, France, May 1918

14
SE 5a D3511 of Maj R S Dallas, No 40 Sqn, Bruay, France, May 1918

15
SE 5a C1752 of Lt F H Taylor, No 41 Sqn, Marieux, France, March 1918

16
SE 5a F5910 of Capt W G Claxton, No 41 Sqn, Conteville, France,
August 1918

17
SE 5 A4853 of Capt C A Lewis, No 56 Sqn, Liettres, France,
June 1917

18
SE 5a B525 of Lt A P F Rhys Davids, No 56 Sqn,
Estrée-Blanche, France, October 1917

19 and 19A
SE 5a B4891 of Capt J T B
McCudden, No 56 Sqn, Baizieux,
France, February 1918

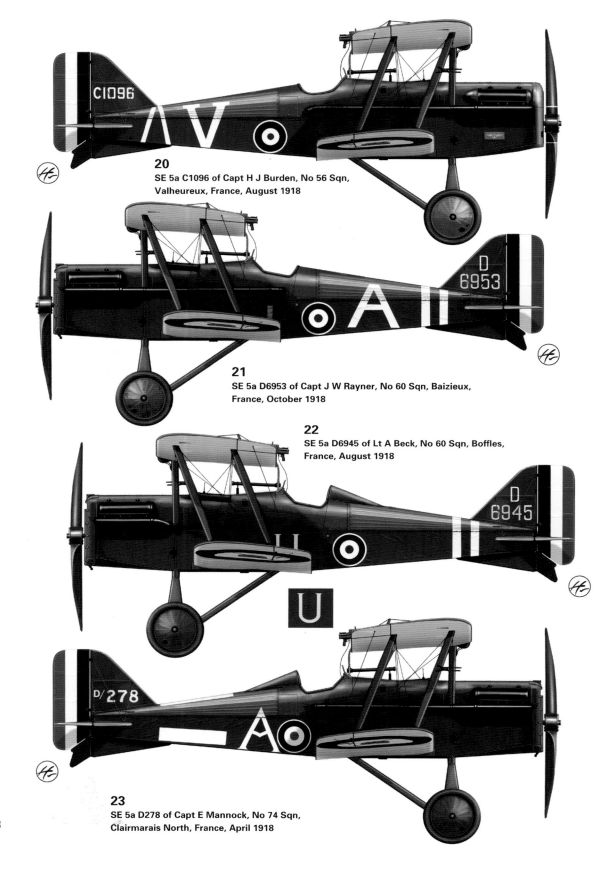

20
SE 5a C1096 of Capt H J Burden, No 56 Sqn,
Valheureux, France, August 1918

21
SE 5a D6953 of Capt J W Rayner, No 60 Sqn, Baizieux,
France, October 1918

22
SE 5a D6945 of Lt A Beck, No 60 Sqn, Boffles,
France, August 1918

23
SE 5a D278 of Capt E Mannock, No 74 Sqn,
Clairmarais North, France, April 1918

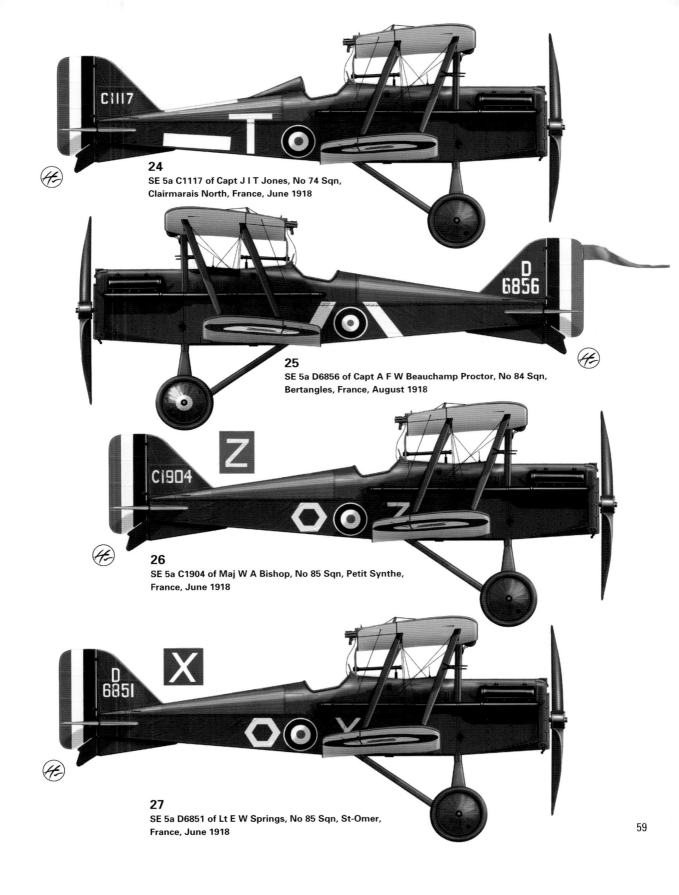

24
SE 5a C1117 of Capt J I T Jones, No 74 Sqn,
Clairmarais North, France, June 1918

25
SE 5a D6856 of Capt A F W Beauchamp Proctor, No 84 Sqn,
Bertangles, France, August 1918

26
SE 5a C1904 of Maj W A Bishop, No 85 Sqn, Petit Synthe,
France, June 1918

27
SE 5a D6851 of Lt E W Springs, No 85 Sqn, St-Omer,
France, June 1918

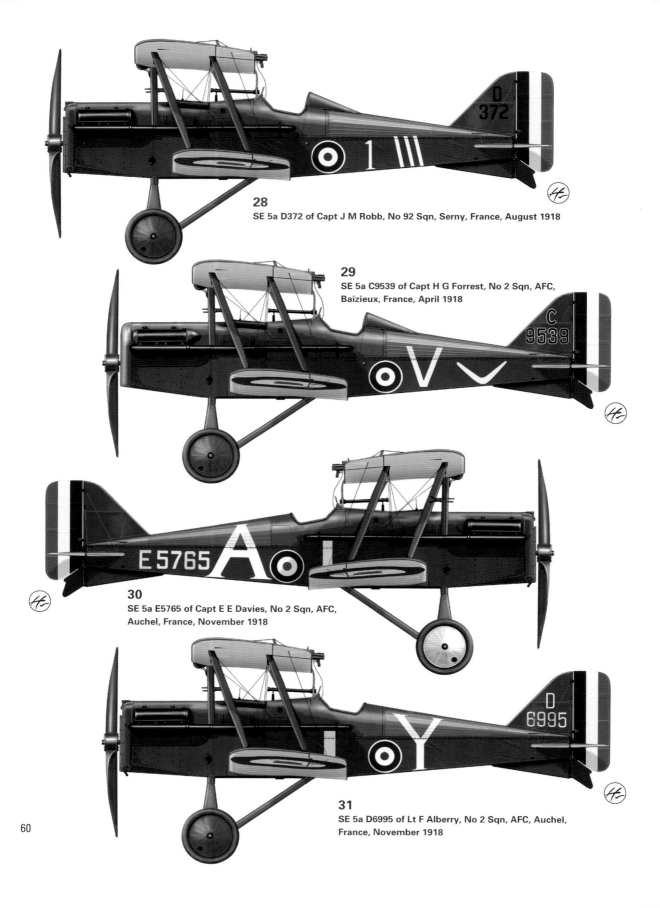

28
SE 5a D372 of Capt J M Robb, No 92 Sqn, Serny, France, August 1918

29
SE 5a C9539 of Capt H G Forrest, No 2 Sqn, AFC,
Baizieux, France, April 1918

30
SE 5a E5765 of Capt E E Davies, No 2 Sqn, AFC,
Auchel, France, November 1918

31
SE 5a D6995 of Lt F Alberry, No 2 Sqn, AFC, Auchel,
France, November 1918

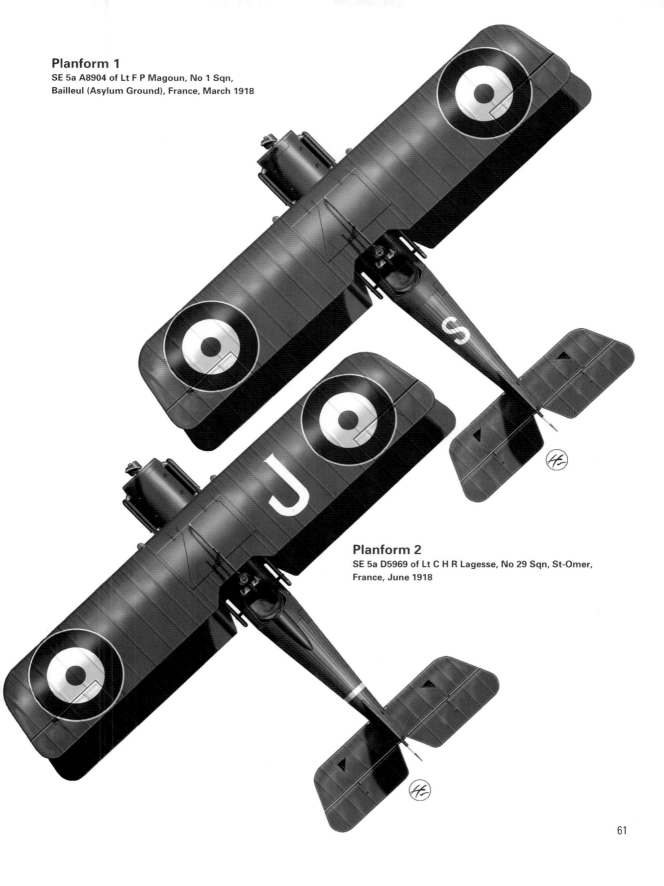

Planform 1
SE 5a A8904 of Lt F P Magoun, No 1 Sqn,
Bailleul (Asylum Ground), France, March 1918

Planform 2
SE 5a D5969 of Lt C H R Lagesse, No 29 Sqn, St-Omer,
France, June 1918

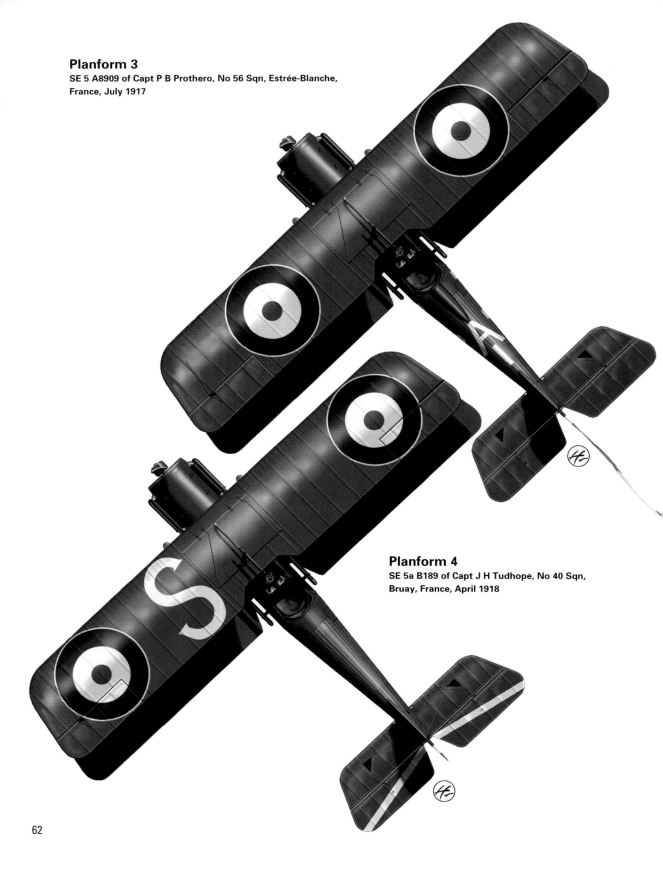

Planform 3
SE 5 A8909 of Capt P B Prothero, No 56 Sqn, Estrée-Blanche, France, July 1917

Planform 4
SE 5a B189 of Capt J H Tudhope, No 40 Sqn, Bruay, France, April 1918

Planform 5
SE 5a D3540 of Capt G H Lewis, No 40 Sqn, Bruay,
France, May 1918

Planform 6
SE 5a B525 of Lt A P F Rhys Davids, No 56 Sqn,
Estrée-Blanche, France, October 1917

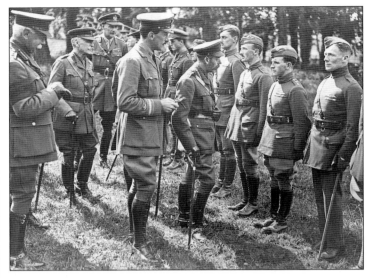

At a presentation near Nieppe Château on 6 August 1918, His Majesty King George V talks to No 74 Sqn's Capt J I T Jones, who that very morning had brought down his 36th and 37th victories. To Jones' right is Capt B Roxburgh-Smith (22 victories) and on his left is Capt S Carlin (10 victories), who had a wooden leg and was nicknamed 'Timbertoes' (*Bruce Robertson*)

100 yards before returning the compliment. The pilot immediately stuck the nose of his machine down and dived steeply with his engine full on – as I hoped he would. By doing so it was impossible, owing to the rush of air, for his observer to fire.

'I went after him full out, firing short bursts. At 10,000 ft he pulled out of the dive, no doubt thinking I had given up the chase, as we were now many miles on his side of the lines. He soon found he was wrong, and I took advantage of his hesitation to fire another good burst. Down in a dive he went again, and I closely followed. Eventually, the machine landed in a large field. The occupants remained in their machine and I fired at them several times before returning to our lines.

'What a trip it was! Hell seemed to be let loose all the way. Flaming anti-aircraft bursts, chains of "flaming onions", and a veritable chatter of rifle and machine gun fire accompanied my journey back to our side.'

Although by 1918 the sky was too dangerous for lone patrols unless the pilot was both confident in his abilities and very experienced, 'Taffy' frequently flew such missions, as he detailed in one of the books he wrote post-war about his experiences with No 74 Sqn;

'I was made a flight commander in June, having taken over from Mannock after he had been promoted to major and put in command of No 85 Sqn. Although I had not lost a single pilot while leading a patrol, I felt like having a peep at things on "the other side" occasionally on my own about dawn.

'There were many advantages in those early morning personal trips, which I used to make very frequently. By setting off very soon after dawn, when the sky was cloudless, I was able to take advantage of the strong glare of the rising sun. Flying very high – at about 19,000 ft – east of the German aerodromes, it was possible to watch any enemy machine in the intense glare. It had another advantage. By flying so high I was out of reach of the German anti-aircraft guns, which did not trouble to fire, and so disclose my presence to the unobservant.'

Flying one of these missions on 6 August 1918, Jones spotted a formation of nine Fokker D VIIs near Sailly sur la Lys and attacked them from the east, as the German pilots had not bothered to look behind them into the sun. To his chagrin he found he had failed to cock his guns and had to break off. As he circled round, wondering if he should try again or wait until the Germans flew closer to the lines, Jones spotted an RE 8 nearby, which prompted two of the Fokkers to head down towards the lone reconnaissance aircraft;

'The time for action on my part had come, and it had to be quick if I was to save the RE 8 crew. I dived with full throttle after the Germans in a state of tremendous tension.

Maj E 'Mick' Mannock VC DSO and two Bars MC served with Nos 40, 74 and 85 Sqns. He was a flight commander whilst with No 74 Sqn, and claimed 36 of his 61 victories with the unit between 12 April and 17 June 1918. Mannock was a man of enormous intensity, as suggested by this photograph, and following internment in a Turkish prison at the start of the war, he possessed an increasingly deep hatred for the Central Powers of Germany, Austria-Hungary and Turkey (*Bruce Robertson*)

After notching up five victories during August and September 1918 flying SE 5as with No 74 Sqn, 1Lt Fred E Luff DFC transferred to the USAS's 25th Aero Squadron (*E F Cheesman*)

'Fortunately for the pilot in the RE 8, he saw the approaching Fokkers and hastily dived for our lines. This gave me time to close up on the Fokkers, which were flying very close together. I opened fire when I was 200 yards behind them, as I feared they would get a long shot home on the RE 8, and I was therefore anxious to distract their attention. I succeeded.

'On hearing the rattle of my machine guns and seeing my tracer and Buckingham bullets flash past, the leading enemy pilot made a sharp turn to the left, which brought him into collision with his compatriot. The craft became firmly interlocked, and then developed a weird flat spin. I could see the pilots struggling as I dived, and fired into the already doomed mass. There was a streak of ominous smoke, followed by a tongue of flame, and soon both craft were enveloped in a blaze which must have quickly ended the agonising moments of the German pilots.'

Despite serving with No 74 Sqn until war's end (he was its CO between November 1918 and February 1919), Jones did not add to his tally after 7 August. Post-war, he volunteered for service in North Russia in 1919, and subsequently remained in the RAF until 1936. Just as war was about to start again, Jones was made a group captain and put in charge of training fighter pilots. He wrote several books on his war experiences, and about his hero 'Mick' Mannock, and in later life could be easily inveigled to talk about World War 1 in his local pub. 'Taffy' Jones died in August 1960 following a fall from a ladder at his Glamorgan home.

As previously mentioned, Jones' flight commander, Maj 'Mick' Mannock, claimed 36 victories with No 74 Sqn, the veteran ace being revered by all those that flew with him in the unit. Having celebrated his 31st birthday in May 1918, he was older than most fighter pilots in action during this period. The son of a serving NCO in the army, he had been born in Aldershot, in Hampshire, in May 1887. Working as a telephone engineer in Turkey when war was declared, he was interned as an enemy alien until repatriated with a serious illness in 1915.

Upon his recovery, Mannock joined the Royal Army Medical Corps, before receiving a commission and transferring to the Royal Engineers in 1916. Despite a congenital defect that left him virtually blind in his left eye, Mannock was accepted by the RFC for pilot training in August 1916 – one of his instructors was none other than James McCudden. In April 1917 he joined No 40 Sqn, and after a slow start, he had claimed 15 victories by September. His final success with the unit came on New Year's Day 1918, and he returned to the Home Establishment a short while later.

In February 1918 Mannock was assigned as a flight commander to No 74 Sqn, which would prove to be a real bonus for the new unit, as he quickly imparted his experience and flair for combat to the younger, newer, pilots in his charge. Once in France, Mannock led by example, claiming 36 victories between 12 April and 17 June (including four on 21 May), to which he would add another eight when given command of No 85 Sqn in mid-June.

Mannock flew D278 'A' when No 74 Sqn went to France, then C1112 in mid-May, before returning to D278 for the rest of that month, followed by C6468. With D278 he achieved 17 victories, five with C1112 and then at least nine with C6468. D278 was finally destroyed when it was hit by a landing Camel at Clairmarais North on 2 June.

'Taffy' Jones wrote a biography of Mannock entitled *King of Air Fighters* in 1934, and in it he reported that Mannock had scored 73 victories – one more than 'Billy' Bishop's hotly disputed 72! We shall read more about Mannock in the No 85 Sqn section.

Jones was a direct beneficiary of the tactics devised by Mannock and put into practice by No 74 Sqn, and he details some of these techniques in the following extract from *King of Air Fighters*;

'Edward Mannock was the first airman on our side, as Boelcke was the first of the enemy, to realise the supreme importance of applying tactics to formation fighting. Our higher command, divorced from actual experience, was stupefied by such brilliant pilots as Ball, Rhys Davids and McCudden, and took some time to realise that a new and audacious fighter had arisen, whose tactics and methods were to prove such a leading factor in the effectiveness of air fighting.

'His tactics when attacking low-flying two-seaters were those of the hawk. He would hover about the sky thousands of feet above his prey, pretending that he was not watching them. Then, when he was quite satisfied that his enemy was off his guard, he would go swooping down at terrific speed to effect a complete surprise. He would flatten out about a mile east of his opponent, and throttling back to steady his machine, he would approach from beneath his victims, having in the meantime reduced his speed to about 100 mph. His favourite shot at a two-seater was a right-angle one, which is the most difficult shot of all.

'His tactic was to compel the enemy to fly into the bullets by aiming a short distance ahead of his target, and holding his fire until the enemy's engine appeared in his sights. If this first burst failed, he would repeat the attack. It was a lucky enemy who did not fall victim to Mannock's guns once he got his sights trained on him. Mannock invariably sighted his own guns, and invented a pet sight of his own. He placed gunnery before flying as a means of gaining victories. "Good flying has never killed a Hun yet", he told his pilots. "You just get on with sighting your guns, and practise spotting Huns. Then shoot them down before they shoot you".

'Mannock had wonderful long eyesight, in spite of the defect in his left eye. He was never surprised during his whole career as a patrol leader. This was one reason why every pilot felt so secure when following him on offensive patrols many miles over enemy territory.'

The third-ranking ace within No 74 Sqn with 22 victories was Capt Benjamin 'Dad' Roxburgh-Smith DFC and Bar CdG, who was even older than Mannock. Born in April 1884, he was working in Lee, southeast London, as a bank clerk when war was declared. Roxburgh-Smith joined the RFC in August 1916 and was posted to No 60 Sqn in France in 1917. However, he was injured in a Nieuport Scout crash before he could see any action, and returned to the UK to recuperate. Following a period as an instructor, Roxburgh-Smith was sent to the newly formed No 74 Sqn and became a part of Mannock's flight.

Despite not claiming his first victory until after he had turned 34, Roxburgh-Smith downed 22 aircraft through to 14 October. He was himself shot down and slightly wounded on 19 July, keeping him out of action for almost three weeks. Roxburgh-Smith was made a flight commander upon recovering from his wounds, and he claimed a trio of Fokker D VIIs on 14 October to bring his scoring to an end. Leaving the

service in 1919, Roxburgh-Smith remained in aviation, and in the 1930s he managed Salisbury aerodrome, in Rhodesia.

No 74 Sqn's only wartime CO in France appears next on the list of the unit's high scorers. Maj Keith L 'Grid' Caldwell MC, DFC and Bar CdG joined the squadron in March 1918, and remained in command until relieved by 'Taffy' Jones nine months later. Born in Wellington, New Zealand, in October 1895, he had joined the local Territorial Infantry in 1914 and then taken lessons at a private flying club the following year – Caldwell took his 'ticket' after just three hours of tuition in a Caudron! Sailing to England in December 1915, he joined the RFC five months later, and had his wings by July 1916. Assigned to No 8 Sqn, he achieved his first victory on 18 September 1916 flying a BE 2d.

Caldwell succeeded in being posted to Nieuport Scout-equipped No 60 Sqn two months later, and he claimed a further eight victories with this unit between 11 December 1916 and 15 September 1917. His final success was scored whilst flying one of the first SE 5as issued to No 60 Sqn, after which he was sent home to the UK to rest. Returning to France with No 74 Sqn in late March 1918, Caldwell would down a further 16 aircraft whilst leading his unit into action over the Western Front.

Although never shot down by the enemy, he came close to death on 5 September 1918 when his aircraft (D6864) was struck by the SE 5a flown by fellow No 74 Sqn ace Capt Sydney Carlin MC DFC DCM during a dogfight. Heading down in what became a right-hand semi-flat spin, his squadronmate (and eight-victory ace) Lt G R Hicks DFC endeavoured to escort him through enemy fighters. At 5000 ft Hicks watched in horror as Caldwell's left leg came out of the cockpit and he placed his foot on the port wing. He then grabbed a cabane strut with his left hand and continued to jiggle the joystick with his right.

Hicks, certain of the imminent death of his CO, and not wanting to witness it, flew away, but Caldwell somehow managed to skim over the

Capt Benjamin 'Dad' Roxburgh-Smith DFC and Bar CdG was No 74 Sqn's third-ranking ace with 22 victories

A true combat veteran, Maj K L 'Grid' Caldwell DFC and Bar MC scored 16 SE 5a victories while leading No 74 Sqn in 1918. He had previously claimed a single success with No 8 Sqn in 1916 and eight victories with No 60 Sqn the following year

High-scoring aces from No 74 Sqn relax between patrols in the early summer of 1918. These men are, rear row, from left to right, Capts B Roxburgh-Smith (22 victories) and A C Kiddie (15 victories), and front row, left to right, Majs 'Mick' Mannock (61 victories) and K L Caldwell (25 victories), unknown, and Capt W E Young (11 victories)

trenches, then, just feet above the ground, jumped for his life. After a couple of somersaults, he picked himself up and dived into the nearest trench, whereupon he asked politely if he could use the telephone!

'Taffy' Jones wrote about Caldwell in a newspaper article published in the 1930s;

'Caldwell had an amazing flair for air fighting, which he usually treated in the most inconsequential manner. Where and how he found the enemy mattered little to him, so long as there was a fight. He never worried a hoot about tactics. So long as there were Germans in the air, "Grid" was happy. No personality in the RAF, including VC winners, had made such an indelible impression on all those who knew the various aces as "Grid" Caldwell.'

Returning to New Zealand to farm after the war, he continued flying until World War 2. Caldwell then undertook various training and administrative duties within the Royal New Zealand Air Force (RNZAF), eventually becoming AOC RNZAF HQ in London. Leaving the service as an air commodore, he returned to farming and eventually died in November 1980.

Like Caldwell, 15-victory ace Capt Andrew C 'Old Man' Kiddie DFC and Bar CdG was also from the dominions, being born in Kimberley, South Africa, in November 1889. Another 'veteran' in terms of his age when he joined No 74 Sqn, he had served with the 18th South African Mounted Rifles in West Africa early in the war. Travelling to England in 1916 to join the RFC, Kiddie was posted to DH 5-equipped No 32 Sqn in the spring of 1917, and claimed a solitary victory with the unit on 20 July that same year.

Kiddie returned to the Home Establishment to instruct upon the completion of his tour in late 1917, and amongst his students was 'Taffy' Jones. He followed the latter to No 74 Sqn prior to the unit heading to France, and one of his first actions almost proved to be his last. On 8 May 1918, the patrol in which Kiddie was a member ran into Fokker Dr Is from *Jasta* 26 during an early offensive patrol near Zillebecke Lake. Although the South African's SE 5a was badly shot up, he was the only squadron pilot to make it back to base. Two others put their damaged scouts down safely elsewhere and two more were killed.

Putting this setback behind him, Kiddie went on to 'make ace' by month-end, and score a total of 14 victories with the SE 5a whilst serving with No 74 Sqn. He had also been promoted to flight commander by war's end.

The last ace to claim a double figure score with the SE 5a whilst flying with No 74 Sqn was Capt Sydney Carlin MC DFC DCM, who was briefly mentioned earlier in this chapter for his collision with his CO, Maj Caldwell. Born in Hull, Yorkshire, in 1889, he had been a farmer pre-war

Despite having lost a leg fighting in the trenches in 1916, Capt Sydney Carlin MC DFC DCM scored ten victories with No 74 Sqn in 1918

prior to joining the Royal Engineers. Carlin won the Distinguished Conduct Medal in 1915 and received a commission in 1916. Later that year, he and his men were forced to hold a trench that they had just finished digging when it came under attack. Badly wounded during the action, he subsequently lost a leg.

Issued with a wooden leg, Carlin was unable to return to the front in such a condition. However, he was determined to continue fighting the Germans, so he decided to transfer to the RFC, and was trained as a pilot. Carlin proved to be such a gifted aviator that he was retained as an instructor until posted to No 74 Sqn in late May 1918. With his new unit's liking for nicknames, it comes as no surprise to find that he was quickly dubbed 'Timbertoes'. Having only one leg did not slow Carlin down when it came to air combat, and between 13 June and 15 September he claimed five aircraft and five kite balloons destroyed – at least five of these victories were achieved in SE 5a D6922.

Having struggled home after his mid-air collision with Maj Caldwell on 5 September, Carlin's luck finally ran out 16 days later when he became the second of six victims claimed by *Jasta* 29 ace Siegfried Westphal. Spending the final weeks of the war as a PoW, Carlin moved to Kenya to farm in 1919, and did not return to the UK until 1939.

He duly re-enlisted in the RAF as an air gunner, and saw combat in Defiant nightfighters. Carlin also managed a few trips as a rear gunner in a Wellington, flying operations over Germany with Sqn Ldr Percy Pickard of the film *No Moon Tonight* fame, as he had known him in Kenya. He then served with Defiant-equipped No 151 Sqn, but was killed during an air raid on the unit's Wittering base, in Cambridgeshire, on 9 May 1941.

No 29 Sqn

A month after No 74 Sqn made its move to France, No 29 Sqn became the last of the old DH 2/Nieuport Scout units to switch to the SE 5a. In fact this squadron had operated French fighters longer than any other British unit, having received its first Nieuport 16s in March 1917 and having retired its last Nieuport 27s in April 1918. No 29 Sqn spent just over six weeks working up with its SE 5as at St-Omer, prior to being posted to Vignacourt, north of Amiens, in early June 1918.

The unit would see considerable action during the final five months of the war, with 15 pilots achieving ace status in the SE 5a by Armistice Day.

The first claim made by No 29 Sqn with the aircraft came on 6 June, when future 20-victory ace Lt (later Captain) C H R Lagesse DFC and Bar CdG brought down a new Fokker D VII behind British lines north of Hazebrouck. Its pilot, Hans Schultz of *Jasta* 18, was duly captured. Two Pfalz D IIIs were also claimed as destroyed later that same day.

The squadron's top scoring ace with the SE 5a was Capt Thomas S Harrison DFC and Bar CdG with 22 victories to his name. Born in King William Town, South Africa, in January 1898, he had served with an artillery regiment during the German East Africa campaign, prior to joining the RFC in April 1917. Posted to No 29 Sqn in May 1918, just as the unit was in the midst of switching to the SE 5a, Harrison claimed his first victory on 27 June and his last on 10 November – the day before the Armistice ended World War 1.

Capt C H R Lagesse DFC and Bar CdG got 20 victories with No 29 Sqn

His skill brought him the DFC and Bar as well as the Belgian CdG. Harrison earned his DFC on 8 July when he shot down an LVG two-seater that was performing 'wireless duty' over the front, then despatched one of its two escorting Pfalz D IIIs for good measure (these were victories three and four). In the citation for the Bar to his DFC, Harrison was described as 'Bold in attack, skilful in manoeuvre, this officer never hesitates to engage the enemy, however superior in numbers'.

One of Harrison's machines was E5947, in which he scored seven of his victories. Like so many aces' aircraft during the war, this SE 5a was flown by another pilot while Harrison was on leave, and he duly destroyed it when the scout was run into a ditch after landing too fast.

Harrison survived the war and returned home, and he later served as a major in the intelligence section of the SAAF in World War 2.

Two pilots claimed 20 victories in SE 5as with No 29 Sqn, namely Capts Camille Henri Raoul Lagesse DFC and Bar CdG and Charles G Ross, who was awarded the same decorations. Like Harrison, they too hailed from foreign lands.

Irreverently nicknamed 'large-arse', Lagesse was born in Quatre Borneo, on the island of Mauritius, in January 1893. He received his education at the Royal College on the island, and at the University of Bordeaux, in France. Trained as a chemist, he worked in a sugar factory prior to travelling to England and joining the 28th London Regiment in 1916. Lagesse transferred to the RFC in July 1917 and was posted to No 29 Sqn in March 1918.

Capt C G Ross DFC and Bar also scored 20 victories with No 29 Sqn

Capt C G Ross claimed his 20th, and last, victory in this SE 5a on 10 November 1918. Note that its serial has been applied twice, and the small size of the 'H' on the top wing (*L A Rogers*)

Making his first claim on 22 May, and attaining ace status on 6 June (all these victories came in D5969), he really hit his straps in the first two weeks of October when he downed eight aircraft and a balloon in E4084 – another pilot ran this aircraft into a hedge whilst overshooting the landing area after Lagesse had left the squadron.

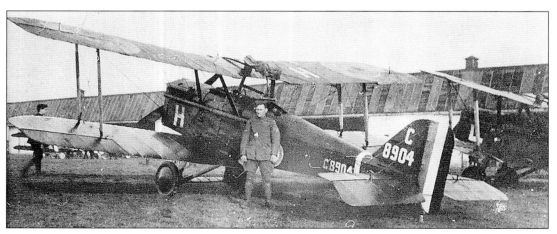

Lagesse spent some time in the flight commanded by ace Capt Hugh G White, who provided me with the following description of him in a letter that he wrote to me many years ago;

'Lagesse was quite a character, and from the moment of joining the squadron was obsessed with thoughts and ideas for shooting down enemy balloons. I certainly gave him plenty of practice up to the time I left the squadron, and I believe he kept up the good work.'

Indeed, he included three kite balloons in his tally of 20 victories. By mid-October Lagesse was physically exhausted, having flown 426 'war' hours, and he was sent back to the UK for a rest. One assumes he returned to his former work as a chemist post-war, and his name appears in the RAF's Officers' List for late 1940 when he joined the Volunteer Reserve.

Capt Charles Ross, who was born in Johannesburg, South Africa, in March 1892, 'made ace' on the same day as Camille Lagesse – 6 June 1918. Joining the RFC in August 1917, he too was sent to No 29 Sqn in March 1918. Three times he scored two kills on one day, and two kite balloons were also included in his score. Ross' DFC and Bar citations mention 'a bold and skilful airman' and 'a fine fighting pilot and leader'. He claimed victories in 11 different SE 5as, with six of them being scored in C9071 in August 1918 – fellow ace Tom Harrison later scored two more successes with this aircraft, including his last one on 10 November.

Immediately post-war, Ross served with the occupation forces in Germany, and in 1921 he joined the SAAF. He eventually retired after World War 2 with the rank of brigadier.

Fellow South African Capt Arthur E Reed DFC and Bar scored 19 victories with No 29 Sqn. Born in Pretoria in August 1898, he too had seen war service in German East Africa with the army (from June 1915 to August 1916), prior to joining the RFC in April 1917. Amongst the pilots posted to No 29 Sqn in March 1918, Reed destroyed 18 aircraft and a single kite balloon between 28 May and 13 September. Eleven of his victims were two-seaters, and six of these were trench-strafing Halberstadts and Hannovers of the *Schutzstaffeln*.

Reed claimed his last seven victories in E4000, and had earlier downed at least five in C1942. E4000 was lost to flak over Ploegsteert on 20 September after it had been passed on to Capt Ross.

By then Reed had been sent back to the UK to rest, and he did not rejoin No 29 Sqn until 1919, by which time it was based in Bickendorf, in Germany. His brother, Company Quarter Master C V Reed, won a VC with the 4th South African Infantry Brigade.

Capt Cristoffel Johannes Venter DFC and Bar was yet another South African to enjoy success with No 29 Sqn, claiming 16 victories with the SE 5a. Born in November 1892, and known as 'Boetie', he made his way to England in early 1917 to join the RFC, and after training was posted to the unit in April 1918. Venter's scoring run of 16 victories between 16 May and 14 August was ended four days after he had claimed his final success when the gunner of a two-seater that he was attacking hit his SE 5a (D6965) over Kemmel, forcing him to crash-land in enemy territory. The ace was captured, and spent the rest of the war as a PoW.

Venter had claimed five of his victories in C1116, which had previously been used by No 74 Sqn ace Maj W E Young DFC to down two of his eleven successes.

Capt A E Reed DFC and Bar scored 19 victories with No 29 Sqn

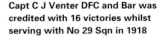

Capt C J Venter DFC and Bar was credited with 16 victories whilst serving with No 29 Sqn in 1918

Post-war, Venter joined the SAAF, and by the beginning of World War 2 he was Officer Commanding Cape Command. Promoted to the rank of major-general, he became Director-General of Air Services. Before his death in February 1977, Venter had become a Director of South African Airways and a Director of the English Electric Company of South Africa.

The highest scoring Canadian SE 5a ace to serve with No 29 Sqn was Capt Ernest C Hoy DFC, who claimed 13 victories in just under eight weeks. Born in Vancouver in May 1895, he had actually joined the squadron in January 1918, but had not made any claims prior to being hospitalised in May. Hoy returned to the unit three months later, and anxious to take the fight to the enemy, he claimed six aircraft and a kite balloon destroyed between 12 and 24 August. Another kite balloon and five more aircraft fell to his guns in September, his tally including three double victories in single actions.

Hoy's luck finally deserted him on 28 September, when he became the fourth victim of seven-victory ace Josef Raesch of *Jasta* 43. Raesch himself had been lucky back on 25 July, when he was shot down by eight-victory ace Lt I F Hind of No 40 Sqn in SE 5a C5358. The German was saved from certain death in his burning Fokker D VII when he used one of the new parachutes recently issued to *Jasta* pilots.

Prior to his demise, seven of Hoy's victories had been claimed in D6939, with fellow ace Charles Ross scoring one of his kills in it too. Just 48 hours before he was shot down, Hoy had had the radiator of D6939 shot through, forcing him to stick the fighter's nose into a trench when he made an emergency landing.

Released from prison camp soon after Armistice Day, Ernest Hoy returned home, and on 7 August 1919 he flew the first airmail flight over the Canadian Rockies in a Curtis JN-4 Jenny. Later, he worked in insurance in the 1920s, then moved to America, living in Clarkesville, Tennessee, where he and his wife raised prize Angus cattle. In 1981 Hoy attended the Aces Reunion in Paris, but died the following April a few weeks short of his 87th birthday.

Seen in factory finish prior to being sent to France, SE 5a D6940 was flown by No 29 Sqn aces Lts H C Rath DFC and C M Wilson DFC, who between them claimed seven victories with it (*Bruce/Leslie*)

Fellow Canadian Lt Henry Coyle Rath DFC scored 12 victories with No 29 Sqn. Born in Tweed, Ontario, in November 1898, he had joined the RFC in September 1917 and was sent to the unit as a replacement pilot on 5 June 1918. Rath's 12 victories were achieved between 28 July and 14 October. At least eight of his victories were claimed in E5964. Sadly, Rath collided with another SE 5a from No 29 Sqn at 12,000 ft over Tournai on 26 October and died from his injuries the next day. The other pilot also lost his life.

The highest scoring Briton to fly SE 5as with No 29 Sqn was 12-victory ace Capt Francis J Davies DFC, who was born in Warwickshire in October 1889. Joining the RFC in May 1917, he had earned his wings by August and was eventually posted to No 29 Sqn. The unit was still flying Nieuports at the time, and Davies claimed one of the last victories for the type in RFC service on 18 March 1918. By the time he scored his next success, on 19 May, he was flying an SE 5a. Davies followed this up with a further four victories by month-end, and by 11 August his score stood at 12 – he had also been promoted to flight commander.

Davies was wounded the following day, and while trying to make it down in one piece, he fainted while still at a height of some 100 ft and crashed. The wounds resulting from this incident effectively ended his war.

Less than three weeks after Francis Davies' crash-landing, another Davies that was destined to be an ace with No 29 Sqn arrived at the unit's Hoog Huis base. Just 19 years old, Lt Edgar George Davies DFC and Bar CdG, from Tufnell Park, north London, had joined the RFC in November 1917. Although only seeing eight weeks of action, he scored ten victories in that time – he destroyed his first aircraft on 16 September and his last on 10 November.

As with several of the citations accompanying awards presented to aces that served with No 29 Sqn, Davies was described, like others had been before him, as 'bold in attack and skilful in manoeuvre. This officer never hesitates to attack the enemy when opportunity occurs, without regard to the disparity in numbers'.

His skill failed him, however, on 6 February 1919, whilst serving with the occupation forces in Germany. Davies crashed at Bickendorf in SE 5a H7162 'E', in which he had scored several of his victories. As he had flown over the airfield, he had attempted a high-speed roll, only for his aircraft to lose both sets of wings. The shattered machine plummeted to the ground like a stone, killing the young ace instantly.

The final ace to achieve a double figure tally was yet another South African – Lt Edgar O Amm DFC and Bar CdG. Born in Johannesburg in August 1898, he had joined the army in South Africa and then travelled to Britain in early 1918 and been seconded into the fledgling RAF. Sent to France to join No 29 Sqn in July, Amm accounted for nine aircraft and one balloon between 12 August and 9 November. Having claimed two Fokker D VIIs in C1141 on the latter date, he was in turn shot down by a third German fighter and forced to spend 48 hours as a PoW.

Amm became a farmer post-war, but when World War 2 broke out he joined the SAAF as a flying instructor. He subsequently saw service in Egypt, the Middle East and in Italy. After the war, Amm sold his farm and founded the South Coast Aviation Company.

Lt E G Davies DFC of No 29 Sqn claimed ten victories. Having survived the war, he was killed in a flying accident in Germany in February 1919 (*E F Cheesman*)

Capt H G White of No 29 Sqn survived a mid-air collision with a Fokker D VII to become an ace with seven victories overall. Four of these were claimed flying SE 5as with No 29 Sqn, whilst the remaining three were scored by White in FE 2ds with No 20 Sqn in 1917

The final No 29 Sqn ace to be detailed in this volume actually only claimed four SE 5a victories with this unit. Capt Hugh White, mentioned earlier in this chapter when giving his impressions of Capt Camille Lagesse, became an ace with No 29 Sqn in May 1918. Born in Maidstone, Kent, in March 1898, he had graduated from Sandhurst and joined the RFC in 1916. Assigned to No 20 Sqn in July of that same year, White had claimed three victories with the FE 2d in April-May 1917. Following a spell as an instructor, he was posted to No 29 Sqn in February 1918, and claimed four victories in five days between 15-19 May. Although White was recommended for a decoration, like so many others, his award write-up probably reached 'higher authority' at the wrong time. His CO's letter of recommendation read as follows;

'This officer has now served as flight commander in this squadron since 26 February 1918. On 17 May he drove down and completely destroyed a hostile machine (in flames) in the vicinity of Merville. On 18 May, he drove down a hostile machine completely out of control, and it was seen to crash in a field about 1 1/2 miles west of Eatafres. On 19 May he destroyed a hostile machine in the vicinity of Bailleul. The following are the facts with regard to the destruction of the last machine mentioned.

'Capt White was leading a patrol at 6000 ft east of Bailleul and encountered nine hostile scouts. Three of his patrol were driven west practically immediately, and Capt White was left alone. He dived on one of the enemy aircraft and fired about 100 rounds at very close range. The enemy aircraft "zoomed" to the left and its top plane caught the leading edge of Capt White's machine, causing the enemy aircraft to turn a cartwheel over his (Capt White's) machine. The shock of the collision flung Capt White forward onto the gun mounting and stopped his engine. The enemy aircraft went down into a dive and Capt White – expecting his machine to break up at any moment – dived after it, firing about 100 rounds.

'The right wing of the enemy aircraft fell off, and it went down completely out of control. Capt White then turned round, and west, to endeavour to re-cross the lines. He was followed back by five enemy aircraft scouts for some distance until these were driven off by friendly machines.

'Capt White managed to keep his machine fairly straight by putting on hard left bank, left rudder and leaning over the side of the cockpit. Near the ground, the machine became uncontrollable, and it crashed on landing near Eecke. The centre section wings of the machine were broken and the right hand planes had anhedral instead of dihedral. The right hand top plane was badly damaged, but the main spars held. The fabric was completely torn off.

'Capt White has led two attacks on hostile balloons, one on 18 and one on 19 May. He drove down one balloon on the 18th, making the observer jump out.'

The unfortunate pilot who collided with White's SE 5a (D3942) was Vzfw Karl Pech of *Jasta* 29, who fell to his death in his Pfalz D III.

I corresponded with Hugh White when he lived near Eastbourne in 1970. In sending me his old CO's recommendation, he added;

'The collision incident occurred when we were shooting up a line of observation balloons. Having seen the nine Pfalz scouts approaching

No 85 Sqn personnel pose for the camera at St-Omer, in northern France, on 21 June 1918. Two notable figures in the pilot line-up are Americans Lts L K Calahan and E W Springs (seventh and eighth from left). Calahan later transferred to the USAS's 148th Aero Squadron and ended the war with five victories, while Springs achieved four victories with No 85 Sqn and eight more with the 148th

Also photographed on 21 June 1918, this anonymous pilot holds up No 85 Sqn's scoreboard

from above, and my chaps having failed to react to my recall/attack red Very signal, I decided to engage them in the hope of keeping them occupied until the rest of my formation followed on and joined in. Unhappily, I collided with one of them, and after this I made for the lines as best I could, followed closely by one enemy aircraft. His guns must have jammed, and his place was taken by yet another.

'I tried seeing what throwing out some remaining Lewis gun ammunition might achieve to lighten my SE 5a. Lo and behold, the very first drum hit and disintegrated the propeller of the following Pfalz, which had just commenced firing! Just then my pilots arrived to see the rest of the Germans off.'

Hugh White stayed in the RAF post-war, and eventually retired as an air vice-marshal in 1955. He passed away in September 1983.

No 85 Sqn

When No 85 Sqn was formed at Upavon, in Wiltshire in August 1917, the unit was originally scheduled to be equipped with Sopwith Dolphins. However, with surplus SE 5as available, the squadron, formed around a nucleus of crews drawn from C Flight of the Central Flying School, equipped with the fighter in May 1918.

No 85 Sqn was led by Canadian ace Maj W A 'Billy' Bishop from Hounslow to France later that month, and following a short

Winner of the VC, DSO and Bar, MC, DFC, *Legion d'Honneur* and *Croix de Guerre*, William Avery Bishop was, controversially, the highest-scoring Canadian ace of World War 1 with 72 victories. This tally saw him ranked first on the list of British and Empire aces (*Bruce Robertson*)

Capt M C McGregor DFC was No 85 Sqn's second-ranking SE 5a ace with ten victories. He had scored his first success flying Pups with No 54 Sqn in 1917

period of working up in the Dunkirk area, the unit was transferred to St-Omer in June.

Historians will make up their own minds about the authenticity of 'Billy' Bishop's 72 victory claims. What is not in doubt is the combat experience he brought to No 85 Sqn when he took command of the unit in March 1918. Bishop already had 47 victories to his credit, plus numerous decorations, including the VC, following his tour with No 60 Sqn in 1917 (see Chapter 1). And although he led the unit in France for just over four weeks, according to his records, between 27 May and 19 June he accounted for 25 aircraft destroyed in SE 5as C6490 (12) and C1904 'Z' (13).

His final five victories all came on 19 June – a day of very little activity according to official British and German records. However, in less than a quarter of an hour he reported downing four Pfalz scouts and a two-seater. Only one *Jasta* lost a pilot that day, and he fell during a balloon attack. As was so often the case, Bishop was flying alone on this patrol, and he knew that the mission would be his last.

The RAF's ranking ace, Bishop was now deemed by Air Force HQ to be too valuable to risk in combat, so he was sent back to the UK to assist in the formation of the Canadian Flying Corps. The war ended before the latter could be sent into action, and Bishop was demobilised and sent home. Rejoining the Royal Canadian Air Force (RCAF) in 1936, he was eventually made Director of Recruiting in 1940. By 1944 Bishop was suffering from ill-health and exhaustion following four hectic years finding new aircrew for the RCAF, so he took early retirement. He eventually passed away in September 1956, aged 62.

Like Bishop, five of the seven remaining pilots to attain ace status with No 85 Sqn had already scored victories with other units. Only one of them made it to double figures, however – New Zealander Capt M C 'Mac' McGregor DFC and Bar, who claimed ten victories. Born in Hunterville in March 1896, he had learned to fly locally in the summer of 1916, and then travelled to England to join the RFC. McGregor was posted to No 54 Sqn early the following year, and he scored his first victory in a Pup on 6 June 1917.

Injured in a crash shortly afterwards and sent back to England, McGregor helped establish a new squadron once fully recovered, and was then posted to the equally new No 85 Sqn as a flight commander. He had gained his second victory before May 1918 was out, and by late October had increased his overall score to 11.

Malcolm McGregor wrote to a friend who was about to fly with the RFC in France about an aerial engagement that he had experienced in August;

'Yesterday morning we had quite a lively scrap with some Fokkers about ten miles from here. They were much keener than usual, and put up such a good scrap that several of our machines were much shot about. I will tell you what happened so that you will know what to expect when you come over.

'We had 11 machines on patrol, A Flight being stationed at 12,000 ft, and five other machines, of which mine was one, up at 17,500 ft. Our job was to help the lower flight, if necessary, and to scrap any Huns that showed up in our vicinity. A dozen Hun machines were further

These SE 5as of No 85 Sqn were built under sub-contract and have had their serial numbers deleted by the censor. 1Lt Elliott White Springs served in No 85 Sqn before going to the 148th Aero Squadron, as did Capt Frank 'Buddy' Hale. Springs' aircraft (D6851) is parked second from the bottom, with an 'X' on its fuselage but a 'T' on the uppersurface of its top wing (*Bruce Robertson*)

Elliott White Springs epitomised the spirit of the young American 'knights of the air' in World War 1. Having trained as an aviation cadet, he became a 16-victory ace, serving with both No 85 Sqn and the USAS's 148th Aero Squadron. After the war he wrote a number of best-selling aviation books, became a multi-millionaire businessman and served in the US Army Air Corps in World War 2 (*Bruce Robertson*)

east, and further off still, too far away to attack, were several more triplanes and Fokker fighters.

'When A Flight dived on some Huns below them, we went down to assist. As we started down, I looked back and saw the enemy machines to the east beginning to come down on top of us. When we arrived in the scrap there seemed to be Fokkers everywhere as, counting the 12 that followed us down, there must have been about 30 of them.

'Some neighbouring SE 5s also joined in, and we had a great old scrap for about 15 minutes. How we avoided collisions I do not know. You would get your sights on a Hun for a second and then have to pull out to avoid being rammed by another SE 5 converging on the same target. I fired at several, but could only be sure of one chap. He was only about

No 85 Sqn pilots Capt S B Horn MC (who claimed seven of his 13 victories with the unit), Lt J Diamond USAS (one victory) and Capt W H Longton DFC and two Bars (11 victories)

Scotsman Capt A C 'Snowy' Randall DFC claimed eight victories serving as a flight commander with No 85 Sqn in 1918. He had previously scored two victories flying DH 2s with No 32 Sqn in early 1917. Prior to joining the RFC, Randall had been wounded fighting in the trenches with the Border Regiment in 1915

Maj 'Mick' Mannock is seen in the cockpit of an SE 5a with no Lewis gun fitted to the Foster quadrant mounting over the upper wing centre section. He claimed nine victories with No 85 Sqn during his brief time as unit CO (*Bruce Robertson*)

30 yards in front, firing at one of our machines, and by some lucky chance I managed to get about 40 rounds right into his cockpit. He went down vertically, completely out of control, and was seen to crash by one of our pilots. Finally, the rest sheered off and we returned home. As we bagged three and the other squadron two, with the loss of only one man from the other squadron, it was quite a good show.'

Returning to New Zealand after the war, McGregor took up farming, but later joined the RNZAF as a squadron leader. Resigning his commission, he switched to commercial flying with Union Airways, only to suffer a broken back in a crash in 1932. McGregor eventually recovered from his injuries and returned to flying, but he was killed in another crash in February 1936 whilst attempting to land at Wellington in a rainstorm.

'Billy' Bishop was replaced as CO of No 85 Sqn in late June 1918 by fellow high-scoring ace Maj 'Mick' Mannock VC DSO and Bar MC and Bar. He arrived on the unit from No 74 Sqn, having already claimed 53 victories. Mannock would achieve an additional nine successes in SE 5a E1295 prior to being brought down in flames in this machine on 26 July 1918 when his fighter was hit by ground fire moments after downing a two-seater near Lestrem. His body was extricated from the wreckage by German soldiers and buried, but his grave was never located with any certainty. Sadly, one of Britain's greatest World War 1 aces has not been granted a place of homage and rest amongst the thousands who fought and died for their country.

When 'Billy' Bishop had joined No 85 Sqn in March 1918, he had brought several pilots with him, including flight commander Capt Spencer B Horn MC. Already an ace, the latter had completed a tour with No 60 Sqn in 1917 when Bishop had been his flight commander. With two victories on Nieuports and four more with the SE 5a, Horn had commanded C Flight after Bishop had left on leave. Born in England on 18 April 1895, just 24 hours after the ship that had brought his parents from Australia to the UK had docked, Horn initially served with the Dragoon Guards early in the war. He transferred to the RFC in 1917, and as mentioned above, enjoyed a successful tour with No 60 Sqn.

Sent home for a rest, Horn spent some months instructing in Ayr, in Scotland, before being asked by Bishop to join No 85 Sqn. He duly added

Capt Oren J Rose DFC and Bar joined the RFC in 1917 and became the top-scoring pilot of No 92 Sqn in 1918 with 16 victories (*E F Cheesman*)

These No 92 Sqn pilots are, in the rear row, from left to right, Lts E F Crabb DFC (six victories), E Shapard (three victories) and Mills, and in the front row, from left to right, Lt Haddon-Smith, Capt O J Rose DFC and Bar (16 victories) and Lt T S Horry DFC (eight victories)

a further seven victories to his tally, bringing his score to 13 by mid-September 1918. After Bishop left in late June, Horn took over his CO's machine – C1904 – and claimed five enemy aircraft with it. This brought the fighter's score to 19. After the war, Horn transferred back to the army and retired as a lieutenant-colonel.

No 85 Sqn's lowest scoring ace was Capt Walter H 'Scruffy' Longton with six victories, although he later claimed five more successes flying SE 5as with No 24 Sqn and finished the war as one of only a handful of airmen to win the DFC and two Bars. Born in Whiston, Lancashire, in September 1892, he had been a car tester pre-war with the Sunbeam Motor Company, and had also enjoyed notable success racing motorcycles.

Longton's first decoration had been an Air Force Cross (AFC), which he received for his work as a test pilot long before he went to France on active duty. However, he eventually got a posting to No 85 Sqn in the spring of 1918 and claimed six victories between 7 July and 22 August. Longton was then posted to No 24 Sqn as a flight commander, where he downed four aircraft and a balloon between 8 and 30 October.

Remaining in the RAF post-war, Longton was promoted to squadron leader in January 1924 and later that year commanded Virginia V bomber-equipped No 58 Sqn. In October 1926 he became an instructor at No 1 Flying Training School at Netheravon, and while taking part in an air race meeting at Bournemouth in June 1927 was killed in a mid-air collision.

No 92 Sqn

The last unit on the Western Front to take the SE 5a into battle was No 92 Sqn, which had originally been formed in London Colney in September 1917 with a nucleus of personnel drawn from No 56 Training Squadron. Equipped with Pups, the unit had remained assigned to the Home Establishment until finally issued with SE 5as in May 1918 and sent to France two months later. It was led into action by Australian Maj Arthur Coningham DSO MC DFC, who had become an ace with No 32 Sqn in 1917 flying DH 2s and DH 5s.

A fighting CO in every sense of the word, Coningham would add four more victories to his tally flying with No 92 Sqn (three in SE 5a D6883) to bring his overall score to 14. After the war he gained high rank with the RAF and a knighthood, but he died in January 1948 when the Avro Tudor in which he was a passenger went missing on a flight to Bermuda.

Despite the war being in its last dreadful months, No 92 Sqn pilots still had plenty of opportunity to claim victories, and the unit created

six aces prior to Armistice Day. Leading the way was Capt Oren J Rose DFC and Bar, who destroyed 16 aircraft between 30 July and 4 November. Born in Platte County, Missouri, in March 1893, but raised in Kansas City, he studied aeronautics at Toronto University prior to heading to the UK to join the RFC in 1917.

Following pilot training, Rose was sent to No 92 Sqn just prior to it going to France. Once in action, he began to score steadily, achieving acedom on 25 August. Rose claimed double victories on three separate occasions, and his DFC citations described him as a 'gallant officer' and 'a brilliant and fearless leader'. Six of his victories were scored in C1142, while other pilots claimed another six successes in this machine, including five for fellow ace Capt W E Reed DFC.

After the war, Rose went with the RAF to Russia, but once discharged he returned to the USA and became a successful businessman in auto parts and sales. He saw further military service in home commands with the USAAF in World War 2 until 1946, then returned to his car business. Eventually retiring in the early 1960s, Rose passed away in Los Angeles in June 1971.

Lt Thomas S Horry DFC was No 92 Sqn's second-ranking ace with eight victories. Born in Boston, Lincolnshire, in May 1898, he had gained his Royal Aero Club Certificate in June 1917. Once trained as a fully-fledged fighter pilot, Horry was posted to France to join No 92 Sqn. Despite the lateness of the war, Tom Horry managed to bag eight victories between 4 and 30 October 1918, although his citation for which he received the DFC firstly mentioned a mission he flew on 5 November. It stated that 'in the face of driving rain and low clouds, he led his patrol far into enemy territory in order to engage enemy troops and transport that were retiring. Reaching his objective, he attacked the enemy with vigour, causing heavy casualties'. Only then did the citation mention his combat victories.

Horry remained in the RAF post-war, becoming a flight lieutenant with No 5 Flying Training School in 1936, and the following year rose to squadron leader rank.

Another of No 92 Sqn's aces to remain in the RAF post-war was Scotsman Capt James M Robb DFC, who was born in Hexham, Northumberland, in January 1895. Joining the Fusiliers upon the outbreak of World War 1, he then transferred to the RFC and joined DH 2-equipped No 32 Sqn following his pilot training. Robb claimed a single victory with the unit in January 1917, but was badly wounded two months later.

Sent back to the UK to recuperate, he eventually joined No 92 Sqn as a flight commander, and scored the unit's first victory on the evening of 22 July 1918 when he downed an Albatros D V. Although slightly wounded on 16 August, Robb ended the war with six victories to add to his solitary DH 2 victory.

Remaining in the RAF post-war, he won the DSO for operations in Kurdistan in the early 1920s, to which he later added an AFC. One of his later positions was AOC Fighter Command in May 1945. Robb rose to the rank of Air Chief-Marshal, being knighted in 1949 and then retiring two years later, having been Inspector-General of the RAF. He retired to Devon and died in December 1968.

Lt T S Horry DFC of No 92 Sqn scored at least six of his eight victories in SE 5a F858

Capt J M Robb DFC of No 92 Sqn achieved six of his seven victories in the SE 5a. His first success came whilst flying a DH 2 with No 32 Sqn in early 1917

THE SE 5a IN THE MIDDLE EAST

Only a handful of units saw action with the SE 5a away from the Western Front, and the first of these was No 111 Sqn. Formed at Deir-el-Ballah, in Palestine, in August 1917 with personnel drawn from No 14 Sqn, the unit flew a mix of aircraft including the Bristol Scout and M 1B monoplane, DH 2, Vickers FB 19 and the F 2B Fighter. It added SE 5as to its inventory in October, before standardising on F 2Bs and SE 5as early in 1918 – a handful of Nieuport Scouts also arrived in January of that year.

SE 5a B139 served with No 111 Sqn in Palestine in 1918 (*L A Rogers*)

No 111 Sqn's highest scoring pilot with the SE 5a was Canadian Capt Austin Lloyd Fleming MC. Born in Toronto in August 1894, the former stockbroker had served with the 1st Battalion, Canadian Railway Troops, prior to transferring to the RFC to train as a pilot. Fleming's first posting, to Pup-equipped No 46 Sqn, came in June 1917, but within a month he had been sent back to England after misidentifying a Nieuport from No 1 Sqn as an Albatros Scout. His burst hit the aircraft, killing its pilot.

At the year's end Fleming was posted out to the Middle East to join No 111 Sqn, and on 17 and 18 January 1918 he claimed two victories in an F 2B Fighter. On the 23rd of that month he scored his first SE 5a success, and by the end of January he had 'made ace' (all three of his victories in the SE 5a came in B538). His fifth victory was over a two-seater, which was captured after its observer force-landed the aircraft behind Allied lines, Fleming's fire having killed the pilot. With another claim in March and two in April, the Canadian brought his overall score to eight. Leaving the RAF in 1919, Fleming returned to Canada, and in World War 2 again served in the RAF. He died in Malaga, Spain, in January 1969.

Lt A L Fleming MC of No 111 Sqn claimed six victories with the SE 5a and two with the F 2B Fighter

The only other pilot to achieve ace status with the SE 5a with No 111 Sqn was Capt Arthur H Peck DSO MC and Bar, who also enjoyed success with the F 2B Fighter. Born in India in April 1889, he had studied at Cambridge and then migrated to Australia in 1908. Returning to the UK in 1914, he became a private in the Devonshire Regiment and was later commissioned into the 10th Battalion. Peck joined the RFC in 1916, and upon learning to fly was retained as an instructor in Egypt.

In August 1917 he became a flight commander with No 111 Sqn, and gained three victories with the F 2B Fighter in October and November. Peck scored his first SE 5a success in December, and then won the MC not for downing hostile aeroplanes, but for forcing three machines to fly back over their lines without completing their mission.

Peck scored four more victories in March 1918, including three on the morning of the 23rd, when he sent two scouts and a two-seater down near Jericho. He remained in the RAF after the war, serving in various 'hotspots', including Iraq in 1928. Promoted to group captain in 1935, he served in the RAF until he retired in 1944. Peck died in the 1970s.

No 17 Sqn

Formed in Gosport in February 1915, No 17 Sqn had been posted to Egypt in November of that year. In July 1916 the unit moved to Mikra Bay, near Salonika, to support operations on the Macedonian front. Flying BE 12 'scouts', which were simply docile BE 2s converted to fighters by covering over the observer's cockpit, as well as Bristol Scouts and DH 2s, the unit had also managed to get its hands on several SPAD VIIs. In late 1917 No 17 Sqn began to receive SE 5as, and its first success with the aircraft came on 22 January 1918 when Capt Franklin G Saunders MC and Bar forced a DFW two-seater to land and be captured.

Born in Swansea in June 1891, Saunders had already claimed four victories in BE 12s with No 47 Sqn, so his first with No 17 Sqn gave him ace status. Unusually, he had earlier served in the RNVR, and had become a Naval Aviator in January 1914 by gaining his Royal Aero Club Certificate. Saunders would claim a total of four victories with the SE 5a.

All of his successes came in B28, which enjoyed a varied life. Following service with No 17 Sqn, it flew with No 145 Sqn (a unit which produced no aces), then No 150 Sqn, where Capt A G Goulding MC DFC CdG gained two more victories with it, as did Lt L Hamilton DFC.

No 17 Sqn's only SE 5a ace was Capt Gerald E Gibbs MC and two Bars Ld'H CdG, who was born in Norwood, south London, in September 1896. Leaving bank employment when war came, he joined the East Surrey Regiment and was later commissioned into the 8th Wiltshires. Gibbs saw service at Suez and on the Turkish border, followed by duty on the North-West Frontier in India in 1915. He was then posted to the Macedonia front, where he requested a transfer to the RFC. Training in Egypt, Gibbs was sent to No 17 Sqn in Macedonia in 1917 and claimed his first victory on 28 January 1918 by destroying a DFW. By early May his score had risen to ten, all with the SE 5a. Later that year he became a flight commander in France with No 29 Sqn, but the war ended before he saw action. Remaining in the RAF post-war, he became a knighted air marshal. Retiring in 1954, Gibbs lived in Kingston, Surrey, and died in October 1992, aged 96.

I met Sir Gerald at his home many years ago, and while he answered some of my questions, he finally told me to refer to his book *Survivor's Story*, and 'quote from it what you like';

'We were doing an escort on the Doiran front for a change, and somehow I had got separated from my flight when I saw a formation of seven enemy fighters (Albatros D IIIs) climbing up at a great pace, doubling their size every time you looked at them. They made me particularly angry because they were coming up cockily and fast, and in such good formation, and I took a dive into them. They were so surprised that they split up and disappeared in all directions, except for the leader, with whom I got tangled at once. He fought well, and we were soon circling round one another right-handed. Our turning circle was very small. We were so close that I had the rare opportunity of actually seeing my adversary face to face. I could see his head in black flying cap and goggles – I could even see him looking at me.

'With my usual "unorthodox trick", I managed to get inside him and underneath, and got my guns to bear. Following a long burst, he flicked right out of the turn to the left. I could see I had hit him hard – it's strange how in your first few fights you aim so carefully and seem

Capt G E Gibbs MC and two Bars poses in front of his No 17 Sqn SE 5a B613. He scored four of his ten victories in this aircraft (*A Thomas*)

to hit nothing, and then suddenly you get the knack and can't miss. He went away down in a steep fast sideslip to the left and then into a very fast spin, and one wing came off. Down he went, spinning faster and faster and slap into Lake Doiran between the lines with a tremendous splash which seemed to go up thousands of feet. I hope he was dead from the beginning – he fought well, and deserved it.

'For some reason the observation posts in our frontlines reported that it was I who had gone in, and my flight was quite shaken when I landed back there a little later. Good excuse for a party!'

The German pilot that Sir Gerald Gibbs had engaged was Ltn Otto Splitgerber, *Staffelführer* of *Jasta* 38 and an eight-victory ace who had earlier flown in France with *Jasta* 12. It was probably the German ace's first encounter with an SE 5a, and he became Gibbs' fifth victory – this engagement had taken place on 13 March 1918.

Sir Gerald Gibbs also wrote about his "unorthodox trick" which he used to such deadly effect in combat when flying the SE 5a;

'We were all taught that a good steady climbing turn would put you in a winning position against another fighter, but personally I did nothing of the sort. As soon as the inevitable circling around any enemy fighter began in order to get one's fixed forward-firing guns to bear, I would tighten the turn as much as possible. A little top rudder would then cause a stall, and the SE 5a would do the first half turn of a spin in the same direction as the circling opponent, and cut across it. Stick forward would straighten her up and stick right back would sit her momentarily on her tail – and I would get in a quick squirt upwards at the enemy fighter as it came past. Then, of course, a sort of tail slide or similar chaos would follow, and if I hadn't hit him hard, something violent was indicated to stop him getting me from above.

'The SE 5a was really very good for its day. Fast (about 130 mph), manoeuvrable, reliable and with a good rate of climb, we were delighted with the fighter. I used to get mine up to 20,000 ft sometimes. We had no oxygen, but we were only at such heights for a few minutes. We also lacked parachutes, armour, self-sealing tanks and a radio – if we'd had them, we'd have had no performance, and would have been "sitters", so we were better off without all these later developments. So, there we sat with our flimsy unprotected petrol-tanks under our seats or behind our dashboards, and being young, thought little of it.'

No 150 Sqn

In April 1918 Nos 17 and 47 Sqns merged their fighter flights at Kirec, near Salonika, to become No 150 Sqn. The new unit was primarily equipped with SE 5as, Camels and Bristol M 1C monoplanes. RAF records can be a little confusing when it comes to ascertaining which pilot was flying with which unit on the Macedonian front at this late stage in the war, although the following aces all seem to have been officially in No 150 Sqn.

Airmen of No 17 Sqn come together for a photograph in 1918. The first three from the left, standing, are, Capt A G Goulding MC DFC (nine victories), F G Saunders MC and Bar (eight victories, four with SE 5as) and G E Gibbs MC and two Bars (ten victories) (*E F Cheesman*)

Canadian Capt Gerald Gordon Bell DFC was the leading ace with the unit. Born in Ottawa in June 1890, he had initially spent time in the Canadian infantry, before transferring to the RFC. His first taste of aerial combat came when he served as an observer in FE 2b pushers with No 22 Sqn in France in early 1917. Bell was credited with scoring three victories with this unit, prior to returning to the UK to be trained as a pilot. Posted to No 47 Sqn in Salonika, he claimed one victory on 13 April 1918, followed by a further 12 with No 150 Sqn. The following extract from Bell's logbook detailed the engagement he fought with an Albatros D V soon after dawn on 15 May 1918 which resulted in him claiming his sixth victory;

'On return from our Cestova reconnaissance flight, I noticed a hostile scout over Piravo. We escorted our reconnaissance machines back to our lines, then returned and attacked. I dived on a scout machine of unknown type and fired 150 rounds at point blank range, following him down to 6000 ft. He was then going down vertically, with black smoke coming out of his centre section and side-slipping from side to side out of control. I then broke off the combat and turned and dived on another hostile machine, which dived away before I could get within reasonable range.'

Surviving the war, Gordon Bell returned to his native Canada, and in the 1960s lived in Brockville, Ontario.

Fellow Canadian ace in 1918 Lt Charles Duncan Bremner Green DFC Ld'H also saw action with both Nos 47 and 150 Sqns. Born in Toronto in August 1897, he initially served with the 164th Battalion of the CEF, before switching from the infantry to the RFC in 1917. Trained as a pilot, Green was posted to No 47 Sqn in January 1918, and like Bell, he scored one victory in the SE 5a with this unit. Following No 47 Sqn's merger with No 150 Sqn, his score rose rapidly, and by mid-July Green had claimed 11 victories. Seven of these claims came in June, and six whilst flying SE 5a B695. Bell had earlier gained a victory in this machine, and another pilot would get one more after Green had ended his tour.

Joining the RCAF in World War 2, Green, as a squadron leader, served with No 5 Flying Training School in Ontario until he was killed in a flying accident on 3 October 1941.

No 150 Sqn's third, and last, SE 5a ace was Lt Leslie Hamilton DFC, who first saw combat with No 17 Sqn in early 1918. He claimed a single

Capt G G Bell DFC of No 150 Sqn scored 16 victories, 13 of them with the SE 5a (*E F Cheesman*)

THE SE 5a IN THE MIDDLE EAST

victory with the unit in April 1918 flying an SE 5a, followed by five more once No 17 Sqn's fighter flight had became No 150 Sqn. Hamilton's final victory, on 18 September 1918, was the first Fokker D VII to be identified on the Macedonian front. The citation for his DFC read, in part, 'A gallant and skilful scout pilot who never hesitates to attack enemy formations, however superior in numbers'. Hamilton was lost, along with Col F F R Minchin and Princess Loewenstein-Wertheim, during a non-stop Atlantic record attempt from Dublin on 26 June 1927.

Another ace pilot to serve with No 150 Sqn was F D Travers, although only three of his 12 victories were achieved with the SE 5a. He had scored one victory flying a BE 12 from No 17 Sqn, and after his SE 5a claims, became the only Bristol M 1 ace, with five enemy machines shot down in September 1918. I corresponded with F Dudley Travers in 1968, and he seems to have been in several fights alongside Bell and Green. He wrote of one combat on 1 June 1918;

'During a bombing raid on Cestovo dump, a formation of 12 hostile scouts was encountered. These were engaged by Capt G G Bell and Lt C D B Green, flying SE 5as, and during the fight that followed, the former fired 20 rounds into a Siemens-Schuckert Scout, which burst into flames. Two enemy aircraft then got on to Capt Bell's tail and were attacked by Green from close range. One was seen to go down out of control, with smoke coming from its centre section. The fight was then continued until another enemy aircraft, coming head-on for Green, pulled straight up and then rolled over on its back, going down out of control. A third SE, piloted by yours truly, then turned and joined in the fight. I engaged and fired a long burst into an enemy scout, which dived vertically out of control and crashed north-west of Bogdanci.'

Travers told me that the total number of aircraft downed over the lines by Nos 17, 47 and 150 Sqns was 57, with six more falling inside Allied lines. With one other brought down by an exploding balloon trap (Ltn Rudolph von Eschwege), it brought the total to 99 by including 35 others claimed as out of control – all this for the loss of 23 British aircraft.

Post-war, Travers flew with Imperial Airways, pioneering routes around the globe. Later still, he was with BOAC, before retiring to Kenya.

Canadian ace Capt Acheson Gosford Goulding MC DFC CdG, who was briefly mentioned earlier in this chapter, also enjoyed success in the SE 5a with both Nos 17 and 150 Sqns in the first half of 1918. Born in Manitoba in May 1893, he joined the CAF as an infantryman when war broke out and saw action in Belgium, prior to transferring to the RFC in September 1916. Having received his wings, Goulding joined No 17 Sqn in Macedonia, where he flew mainly BE 12s.

He claimed five victories with this unit in 1918, with the first of these being scored by him in either a Bristol D Scout or a Nieuport Scout – neither type was technically serving with No 17 Sqn at the time, however!

SE 5a B692 of No 150 Sqn was used by Capt G G Bell DFC to score four of his 16 victories. Lt L Hamilton DFC also claimed two of his six successes in it. Note the unusual camouflage on the unidentified aircraft behind the SE 5a (*A Thomas*)

Goulding's remaining four victories came in SE 5a B690. His first two claims (shared with Capt Gibbs) were over DFW two-seaters, both of which came down inside Allied lines. The unit had worked out a system of ground signalling for communicating with its pilots if they were flying over, or near, their home airfield, and these worked a treat for the 20 March 1918 DFW victory, as Gibbs' recalled in his book *Survivor's Story*;

'I was patrolling over our airfield at Marian when suddenly I saw my precious ground strips indicating the height and position of an enemy aircraft. I soon caught sight of him – a two-seater at about 17,000 ft – and climbed up, hidden under his tail.

'When about 20 miles behind our lines, he suddenly spotted me and turned for home – but too late. With me was my "half section", A G Goulding. We always hunted in pairs, and usually stuck to the same pair. Being the leader, I was well ahead, and so was lucky enough to do the first attack. Keeping out of range, I climbed above and ahead of the two-seater and then made a head-on, or rather bow attack, presenting a very difficult shot for the observer with his rear mounting.

'The very first attack crippled the engine, and he started to lose height – but in the direction of his own lines, so I followed just out of range. Then I came in close and was amazed to see that the observer was fluttering a white handkerchief – I realised in the same moment that he would have to land far short of his own lines. This he did, in a pretty good field, as I circled round – but his propeller continued to tick over. Afraid of a trick, I waved the two occupants away from the aircraft, and they obeyed. I then landed alongside, jumped out with my revolver and ran over to them in case they thought of destroying maps or taking off again.'

When flying with No 150 Sqn after the merger, Goulding raised his score to nine by 8 June. His eighth victory had been claimed with B690, which also claimed a solitary success with F D Travers at the controls. C D B Green then crashed it on 12 June, writing the venerable scout off.

Having survived the war, Goulding subsequently died in Winnipeg in April 1951.

Fellow Canadian ace Lt Arthur E DeM 'Jacko' Jarvis DFC CdG also achieved four SE 5a victories with No 150 Sqn in July 1918. Born in Napanee, Ontario, in November 1894, he had been wounded at Vimy Ridge while serving with the East Ontario Regiment, and then transferred to the RFC in August 1917. Serving initially with No 17 Sqn, Jarvis claimed two victories with the Bristol M 1C monoplane in April 1918 soon after No 150 Sqn had been created. He downed a third aircraft in a Camel in May, and then completed his scoring with four SE 5a victories between 11 and 26 July.

'Jacko' Jarvis eventually passed away in his native Canada in January 1969.

Capts G E Gibbs and A G Goulding flank the crew of the DFW they forced down on 20 March 1918

APPENDICES

SE 5/5a ACES

Western Front

Sqn	Name	Score with Sqn	Score with SE 5/5a	Final Tally
No 1 Sqn	Capt P J Clayson MC DFC	29	29	29
	Capt H A Kullberg DFC	19	19	19
	1Lt D Knight	10	10	10
	Capt C C Clark	10	7	10
	Lt B H Moody	9	9	9
	Lt J C Bateman	7	7	7
	2Lt T S Kelly	6	6	6
	Capt H A Rigby	6	6	6
	Lt E E Owen	5	5	5
	2Lt D E Cameron	5	5	5
	Lt K J P Laing	5	5	5
	Lt F P Magoun MC	5	5	5
	Lt K C Mills	5	5	5
	Lt W A Smart	5	5	5
No 24 Sqn	Maj T F Hazell DSO MC DFC*	23	23	43
	Capt I D R McDonald MC DFC	20	17	20
	Capt H D Barton DFC*	19	19	19
	Capt A K Cowper MC**	19	17	19
	Capt W C Lambert DFC	18	18	18
	Capt G E H McElroy MC** DFC*	16	46	46
	Lt H B Richardson MC DFC	15	15	15
	Lt R T Mark MC*	14	14	14
	Lt J J Dawe	8	8	8
	Capt R G Hammersley CdG	8	8	8
	Capt C N Lowe MC DFC	7	9	9
	Lt H B Redler MC	7	7	10
	Capt A J Brown MC	7	5	8
	Capt C Mc G Farrell DFC	7	7	7
	Lt P A McDougall MC	7	6	7
	1Lt H L Bair DFC DSC	6	6	6
	Lt J E A R Daley DFC	6	6	6
	Lt T M Harries DFC	5	5	11
	Capt G O Johnson MC CdG	5	11	11
	Capt W H Longton DFC**	5	11	11
No 29 Sqn	Capt T S Harrison DFC* CdG	22	22	22
	Capt C H R Lagesse DFC* CdG	20	20	20
	Capt C G Ross DFC* CdG	20	20	20
	Capt A E Reed DFC*	19	19	19
	Capt C J Venter DFC*	16	16	16
	Capt E C Hoy DFC	13	13	13
	Lt H C Rath DFC	12	12	12

Sqn	Name	Score with Sqn	Score with SE 5/5a	Final Tally
	Capt F J Davies DFC	11	12	12
	Lt E G Davies DFC* CdG	10	10	10
	Lt E O Amm DFC* CdG	10	10	10
	Capt R H Rusby DFC	10	7	10
	Capt G W Wareing DFC	9	9	9
	Lt C M Wilson DFC	8	8	8
	Lt S M Brown DFC	5	5	5
	Capt R C L Holme MC	5	5	5
No 32 Sqn	Capt W A Tyrell MC	17	12	17
	Capt A A Callender	8	8	8
	Capt J O Donaldson DFC* DSC(US)	7	7	7
	Capt W B Green DFC Ld'H	7	7	7
	Capt F L Hale DFC	7	7	7
	Capt A Claydon DFC	6	7	7
	Lt G E B Lawson DFC	6	6	6
	Lt B Rogers DFC	6	6	6
No 40 Sqn	Capt G E H McElroy MC** DFC*	31	47	47
	Lt L Bennett Jr	12	12	12
	Maj R G Landis DFC DSC(US)	12	12	12
	Capt I P R Napier MC Ld'H CdG	12	10	12
	Capt W L Harrison MC*	11	10	12
	Capt G H Lewis DFC	10	10	12
	2Lt I L Roy DFC	10	10	10
	Capt J H Tudhope MC*	10	8	10
	Maj R S Dallas DSO DSC* CdG	9	9	32
	Capt I F Hind	8	8	8
	Capt G J Strange	7	7	7
	Capt G C Dixon	5	7	9
	1Lt D F Murmann	5	5	5
	Lt J H Wallwork MC	5	5	5
	Lt H S Wolff	5	5	5
No 41 Sqn	Capt W G Claxton DSO DFC*	37	37	37
	Capt F R G McCall DSO DFC MC*	32	32	35
	Capt W E Shields DFC*	24	24	24
	Capt E J Stephens DFC	13	13	13
	Capt F O Soden DFC	11	25	27
	Capt R W Chappell MC	9	9	11
	Maj G H Bowman DSO MC* DFC CdG	8	30	32
	Capt A S Hemming DFC	8	8	8
	Lt F H Taylor MC	8	9	10
	Lt F H Davis	7	7	7
	Lt M P MacLeod DFC CdG	7	7	7
	Lt S A Puffer	7	7	7
	Lt H E Watson	6	6	6
	Capt L J MacLean MC*	5	5	5
	Lt W J Gillespie CdG	5	5	5
No 56 Sqn	Maj J T B McCudden VC DSO * MC* MM CdG	51	51	57
	Capt R T C Hoidge MC*	27	28	28
	Maj G J C Maxwell MC DFC	26	26	26

Sqn	Name	Score with Sqn	Score with SE 5/5a	Final Tally
	Lt A P F Rhys Davids DSO MC*	25	25	25
	Maj G H Bowman DSO MC* DFC CdG	22	30	32
	Lt L M Barlow MC**	20	20	20
	Capt R A Maybery MC*	20	20	20
	Capt H J Burden DSO DFC	16	16	16
	Maj C M Crowe MC DFC	14	15	15
	Lt M E Mealing MC	14	14	14
	Capt A Ball VC DSO** MC	11	9	44
	Capt W R Irwin DFC*	11	11	11
	Capt T Durrant	10	10	11
	Lt R H Sloley	9	9	9
	Capt E W Broadberry MC	8	8	8
	Capt K W Junor MC	8	8	8
	Capt C A Lewis MC	8	8	8
	Lt K K Muspratt MC	8	8	8
	Capt L W Jarvis	7	7	7
	Lt H J Walkerdine MC	7	7	7
	Capt W S Fielding-Johnson MC* DFC	6	6	6
	Capt P B Prothero	6	6	8
	Capt W O Boger DFC	5	5	5
	Capt D W Grinnell-Milne MC DFC*	5	5	6
	Lt C H Jeffs	5	5	5
	Lt H A S Molyneaux DFC	5	5	5
No 60 Sqn	Capt F O Soden DFC	16	25	27
	Capt H A Hamersley MC	13	13	13
	Capt J D Belgrave MC	12	12	18
	Capt A W Saunders DFC	12	12	12
	Capt A Beck DFC	11	11	11
	Capt W A Bishop VC DSO* MC DFC CDG Ld'H	11	36	72
	Capt W J A Duncan MC*	11	11	11
	Lt W E Jenkins	10	10	10
	Capt R L Chidlaw-Roberts MC	9	10	10
	Capt J E Doyle DFC	9	9	9
	Capt G M Duncan DFC	8	8	8
	Capt H G Hegarty MC	8	8	8
	Capt W J Rutherford	8	7	8
	Lt J S Griffith DFC	7	7	7
	Capt J B Crompton	5	5	5
	Capt J W Rayner	5	5	5
	Lt R K Whitney DFC	5	5	5
No 64 Sqn	Capt J A Slater MC* DFC	22	21	24
	Capt E R Tempest MC DFC	17	16	17
	Capt P S Burge MC	11	11	11
	Capt T Rose DFC	11	11	11
	Capt C W Cudemore MC DFC	10	10	15
	Capt W H Farrow DFC	9	9	10
	Capt D Lloyd-Evans DFC	8	8	8
	Lt C A Bissonette	6	6	6
	Lt B A Walkerdine	6	6	6
	Capt E D Atkinson DFC	5	7	10
	Maj R StC McClintock MC	5	5	5

Sqn	Name	Score with Sqn	Score with SE 5/5a	Final Tally
No 74 Sqn	Capt J I T Jones DSO MC DFC* MM	37	37	37
	Maj E Mannock VC DSO* MC*	36	45	61
	Capt B Roxburgh-Smith DFC* CdG	22	22	22
	Maj K L Caldwell MC DFC* CdG	16	17	25
	Capt A C Kiddie DFC* CdG	14	14	15
	Capt S Carlin MC DFC DCM	10	10	10
	Lt F S Gordon DFC	9	9	9
	Lt F J Hunt DFC	9	9	9
	Capt C B Glynn DFC	8	8	8
	Lt G R Hicks DFC	8	8	8
	Maj W E Young DFC	8	8	11
	Lt H E Dolan MC	7	7	7
	Lt H G Clements	6	6	6
	Lt G W G Gauld DFC	5	5	5
	Lt P F C Howe	5	5	5
	1Lt F E Luff DFC	5	5	5
	1Lt H G Shoemaker	5	5	5
No 84 Sqn	Capt A F W Beauchamp Proctor VC DSO MC* DFC	54	54	54
	Capt W A Southey DFC*	20	20	20
	Capt C F Falkenberg DFC*	17	17	17
	Capt R A Grosvenor MC*	16	16	16
	Capt S W Highwood DFC*	16	16	16
	Capt H W L Saunders MC DFC	15	15	15
	Capt J V Sorsoleil MC	14	14	14
	Lt E A Clear MC	12	12	12
	Capt R Manzer DFC	12	12	12
	Lt N W R Mawle DFC	12	12	12
	Capt J S Ralston MC DFC	12	12	12
	Capt F E Brown MC*	10	10	10
	Lt W H Brown MC	9	9	9
	Lt J F Larsen	9	9	9
	Capt K M StC G Leask MC*	8	8	8
	Lt P K Hobson MC	7	7	7
	Lt H O MacDonald	7	7	7
	Lt W J B Nell	7	7	7
	Lt C L Stubbs	7	7	7
	1Lt G A Vaughn Jr DFC DSC	7	7	13
	Capt G O Johnson MC CdG	6	11	11
	Lt J A McCudden MC	6	6	8
	Lt C R Thompson DFC	6	6	6
	Capt J M Child MC OofL CdG	5	5	8
	Lt C F C Wilson	5	5	5
No 85 Sqn	Maj W A Bishop VC DSO* MC DFC CDG Ld'H	25	36	72
	Capt M C McGregor DFC*	10	10	11
	Capt A C Randall DFC	8	8	10
	Maj E Mannock VC DSO* MC*	9	45	61
	Lt J W Warner DFC	8	8	8
	Lt A S Cunningham-Reid DFC	7	7	7
	Capt S B Horn MC	7	11	13
	Capt W H Longton DFC**	6	11	11

Sqn	Name	Score with Sqn	Score with SE 5/5a	Final Tally
No 92 Sqn	Capt O J Rose DFC*	16	16	16
	Lt T S Horry DFC	8	8	8
	Capt W E Reed DFC	7	7	9
	Lt E F Crabb DFC	6	6	6
	Capt J M Robb DFC	6	6	7
	Lt H B Good	5	5	5
No 2 Sqn AFC	Capt F R Smith DFC	16	16	16
	Maj R C Phillipps MC* DFC	14	14	15
	Capt R L Manuel DFC	12	12	12
	Capt H G Forrest DFC	11	11	11
	Capt A T Cole MC DFC	9	9	9
	Capt E D Cummings DFC	9	9	9
	Capt G H Blaxland	8	8	8
	Lt F Alberry DCM	7	7	7
	Capt R W Howard MC	7	7	8
	Capt E E Davies DFC	7	7	7
	Lt J J Wellwood DFC	6	6	6
	Capt R W McKenzie MC	6	5	6
	Capt A G Clark	5	5	5
	Lt G J Cox	5	5	5

Middle East/Macedonian Fronts

Sqn	Name	Score with Sqn	Score with SE 5/5a	Final Tally
No 17 Sqn	Capt G E Gibbs MC** Ld'H CdG	10	10	10
No 111 Sqn	Capt A L Fleming MC	8	6	8
	Capt A H Peck DSO MC*	8	5	8
No 150 Sqn	Capt G G Bell DFC Ld'H	12	13	16
	Lt C D B Green DFC	10	10	11
	Lt L Hamilton DFC	6	6	6

Awards Key

* – Bar (for medal awarded more than once)
VC – Victoria Cross
MM – Military Medal
MC – Military Cross
DFC – Distinguished Flying Cross
DSO – Distinguished Service Order
DSC – Distinguished Service Cross
DSC(US) – Distinguished Service Cross(United States)
DCM – Distinguished Conduct Medal
CdG – *Croix de Guerre*
Ld'H – *Légion d'honneur*
OofL – Order of Leopold

1

SE 5a C1835 of Lt H A Kullberg, No 1 Sqn, Clairmarais South, France, July 1918

American ace Lt (later promoted to captain) Harold Kullberg claimed seven of his 19 victories with this machine between 15 June (when he destroyed his one and only kite balloon) and 9 August 1918. It bears standard RAF camouflage for this late war period, with the squadron's identification mark of a small white circle behind the fuselage cockade and the individual letter 'T' (later changed to 'P'). The aircraft's serial number is stencilled in white on the fin, and its wheel covers have been painted dark blue – the latter was almost certainly a flight marking.

2

SE 5a A8904 of Lt F P Magoun, No 1 Sqn, Bailleul (Asylum Ground), France, March 1918

Another American to 'make ace' with No 1 Sqn in 1918, Lt Francis Magoun scored his first two (of five) victories with this aircraft on 28 February and 15 March – both were shared claims, as was the fashion with No 1 Sqn. A8904 is also finished in standard camouflage, with the squadron marking of two inverted white bars on either side of the cockade and the individual letter 'S' towards the rear of the fuselage. This letter was repeated on the upper fuselage decking (see Planform 1 for details). A veteran of many months in the frontline, A8904 had previously served with Nos 56 and 84 Sqns in 1917, where it had been damaged on at least two occasions in accidents.

3

SE 5a C1106 of 1Lt D Knight, No 1 Sqn, Clairmarais South, France, June 1918

SE 5a C1106 was used by 1Lt Duerson 'Dewey' Knight during the summer of 1918, the American claiming three shared victories with it in early June. One of these was a Fokker Dr I from *Jasta* 40 that he helped to bring down inside Allied lines on the 9th. Again, the aircraft features the No 1 Sqn identification circle, serial number and individual letter 'Y' in white. Fellow No 1 Sqn ten-victory ace Capt C C Clark had earlier claimed two victories with C1106 on 29 April 1918.

4

SE 5a B891 of Capt G E H McElroy, No 24 Sqn, Matigny, France, March 1918

B891 was flown by four No 24 Sqn aces – Capt Reuben Hammersley (who scored two of his eight victories with it), Capt John Ralston (who briefly flew with No 24 Sqn, but claimed all 12 of his victories with No 84 Sqn), Capt G E H McElroy (who downed five aircraft with it) and Peter McDougall (who scored one of his seven successes in B891). The fighter was marked with the individual letter 'T' just aft of the fuselage roundel, while the single white vertical bar for squadron identification ran from the forward edge of the cockpit to the wing root. After mid-March, this marking was changed to two small vertical white bars either side of the roundel, although by then B891 had been lost. Finally, the serial number on the fin was in black, edged in white.

5

SE 5a E1293 of Capt C N Lowe, No 24 Sqn, Conteville, France, July 1918

Capt C N Lowe MC DFC claimed the last of his nine victories in E1293 on 1 July 1918, while Capt Conway Farrell DFC got his fourth kill (of seven) with it on 26 July by helping to bring down a DFW in Allied lines. The aircraft features No 24 Sqn's late war marking of two white vertical bars on either side of the roundel. Note also that the unit had switched from individual letters to numbers for identifying its aircraft by July 1918 – the number was repeated on the top wing, beneath the gun mounting. Lowe denoted his position as B Flight commander by attaching a streamer to E1293's rudder.

6

SE 5a F5459 of Lt T M Harries, No 24 Sqn, Busigny, France, October 1918

Lt Tom Harries DFC gained his 11th, and last, victory with F5459 on 29 October 1918. This machine subsequently featured reduced wing dihedral for a series of test flights performed by the unit. No 24 Sqn reverted back to letters for individual aircraft markings just prior to war's end, and this machine featured a white 'Y' on its fuselage sides and on the top wing beneath the gun mounting. Note also that the scout bore its serial in large white numbers on the rear fuselage and in black across the rudder tricolour. Finally, F5459 was fitted with a non-standard windscreen. Harries was also a flight commander, hence the streamer.

7

SE 5a D279 of Lt H B Richardson, No 24 Sqn, Conteville, France, March 1918

D279 was used by Lt H B Richardson MC DFC to down his last seven of fifteen victories between 17 March and 4 April 1918. Fellow No 24 Sqn ace Capt I D R McDonald MC DFC also claimed his 13th of 20 victories with D279 during a dawn patrol on 16 May 1918. The following month, an unnamed pilot damaged the aircraft's undercarriage so badly in a hard landing that the fighter was struck off charge. Featuring standard squadron markings for the period (with the letter 'A' in white both on its fuselage sides and in the centre of its top wing), D279 bore the presentation name *STEYNSBURG SOUTH AFRICA* in white lettering on either side of its rear fuselage.

8

SE 5a C1942 of Capt A E Reed, No 29 Sqn, Hoog Huis, France, August 1918

Capt Arthur Reed DFC and Bar flew C1942 in July-August 1918 and claimed at least five German aircraft shot down with it. The fighter's only non-standard marking was its slightly stylised individual letter 'A' beneath the cockpit, which was also repeated on the starboard side of the top wing, and in black beneath the port wing. No 29 Sqn's unit marking was a solitary white band encircling the rear fuselage.

9

SE 5a H7162 of Lt E G Davies, No 29 Sqn, Marcke, France, November 1918

H7162 was the regular mount of Lt Edgar Davies DFC and Bar CdG in the autumn of 1918, and he scored three of his ten victories with the aircraft in October and November 1918. The letter 'E' in white below the cockpit was repeated on the uppersurface of the top wing beneath the gun mounting and also on the undersurface of the lower port wing in black. The fighter also had non-standard white wheel covers. Davies was killed in this machine when it shed its wings and crashed during an attempted high-speed roll over Bickendorf airfield on 6 February 1919.

10

SE 5a D5969 of Lt C H R Lagesse, No 29 Sqn, St-Omer, France, June 1918

Lt Henri Lagesse DFC and Bar CdG used D5969 to gain the first five of his victories (out of a final total of 20) in May and June 1918. The fighter featured all the standard No 29 Sqn markings (see also Planform 2), but with a black, rather than white, serial on the fin. By mid-June 1918 this SE 5a was deemed to be worn out and not worth refurbishing, Lt Lagesse receiving E1263 in its place.

11

SE 5a D6991 of Lt B Rogers, No 32 Sqn, La Bellevue, France, September 1918

Californian ace Lt Bogart Rogers achieved two victories in D6991 on 6 September 1918 and his sixth, and last, success on 1 November. Two small inverted white bars aft of the fuselage roundel denoted the fighter's assignment to No 32 Sqn, while the letter 'A' on the fuselage side just ahead of the lower wing's leading edge identified the machine as coming from A Flight. The latter marking was usually repeated on the uppersurface of the starboard wing, while an individual number on the port wing identified the SE 5a itself.

12

SE 5a B189 of Capt J H Tudhope, No 40 Sqn, Bruay, France, April 1918

Three aces claimed victories with No 40 Sqn whilst flying B189. Capt William Harrison MC and Bar was the first, scoring his tenth of twelve victories with it on 26 March 1918. Capt John Tudhope MC and Bar then downed his last two kills in B189 in April 1918 to take his score to ten. Finally, American Maj Reed Landis DFC and Bar DSC(US) achieved his first of an eventual 12 victories in the fighter on 8 May. The aircraft featured the squadron's unique white sloping 'N' identification marking on the rear part of its fuselage. An individual letter 'S' also adorned the fin above the serial number (edged in white), this being repeated in white on the port uppersurface of the top wing (see Planform 4). Two white lines were also painted on the uppersurfaces of the rear wing and elevator.

13

SE 5a D3540 of Capt G H Lewis, No 40 Sqn, Bruay, France, May 1918

Capt Gwilym Lewis DFC scored victories six through to ten in D3540 in April and May 1918. The fighter featured the squadron's forward 'N' marking on the rear fuselage sides, as well as the individual letter 'K' in black, edged with white, just aft of the roundel – the latter marking was also repeated on

the top and bottom wings (see Planform 5 for details). The SE 5a also had white wheel covers, while the interplane struts were painted in black and white sections. Squadronmate Lt C O Rusden also scored a victory in this machine.

14

SE 5a D3511 of Maj R S Dallas, No 40 Sqn, Bruay, France, May 1918

Maj Roderic Dallas DSO DSC and Bar CdG flew D3511 during his two-month tenure as CO of No 40 Sqn in 1918, and he gained at least five victories with it in May. Following the Australian ace's death in combat on 1 June, the fighter was used by fellow aces Capts Gwilym Lewis and G E H McElroy. Indeed, Lewis claimed his last two victories with D3511 in the first week of July. This SE 5a boasted a decidedly non-standard camouflage scheme with no unit markings – even its serial number was partially obliterated by the paintwork, which was almost certainly applied in the field by No 40 Sqn.

15

SE 5a C1752 of Lt F H Taylor, No 41 Sqn, Marieux, France, March 1918

C1752 was used by Lt Frank Taylor MC between 16 and 24 March 1918 to claim seven of his eventual ten victories. The two white vertical bars on either side of the cockade indicate the machine's use by the unit before 22 March 1918, at which time the squadron markings changed to two bars aft of the cockade (see Profile 16). The fighter's individual letter 'E' was painted aft of the two bars. Having experienced much action in the early months of 1918, C1752 was declared war-weary in May and struck off charge.

16

SE 5a F5910 of Capt W G Claxton, No 41 Sqn, Conteville, France, August 1918

No 41 Sqn's ranking ace Capt Bill Claxton DSO DFC and Bar achieved seven of his 37 victories in F5910 in July and August 1918. On the morning of 17 August 1918, Claxton's flight, under the command of fellow high-scoring ace Capt Frederick McCall, encountered the Fokker D VIIs of *Jasta 20* (part of an enemy formation estimated to number as many as 60 fighters) while patrolling the front. In the ensuing battle, Claxton (in F5910) was shot down behind enemy lines by future ace Ltn Johannes Gildemeister. Suffering from a serious head wound, he was captured east of Wervicq – only the immediate skills of a German doctor saved his life. F5910 is shown here in profile in No 41 Sqn's post-March 1918 markings of two white bars aft of the roundel, with the fighter's individual letter 'A' placed between the bars and the rear fuselage. Note also the SE 5a's red wheel covers.

17

SE 5 A4853 of Capt C A Lewis, No 56 Sqn, Liettres, France, June 1917

Amongst the first SE 5s to see action in France, A4853 was the usual mount of early No 56 Sqn ace Capt Cecil Lewis MC. He claimed all eight of his victories with the aircraft between 5 May and 17 June 1917, and squadronmate Capt D S Wilkinson also subsequently scored two successes with it. Rebuilt as SE 5a B4853 and transferred to No 84 Sqn in the late summer of 1917, it claimed one further victory with ace Capt J S Ralston at the controls in October of that year. The fighter was also occasionally flown by fellow No 84 Sqn ace Capt K M StC G Leask. When serving with No 56 Sqn, A4853 bore the code 'C2' (denoting its assignment to C Flight) in white, edged with red – this marking was repeated on the top decking. The aircraft also had its headrest and wheel covers painted red. Finally, note the unusual blue, white and red design encircling the cockpit.

18

SE 5a B525 of Lt A P F Rhys Davids, No 56 Sqn, Estrée-Blanche, France, October 1917

No 56 Sqn's fourth-ranking ace Lt Arthur Rhys Davids DSO MC and Bar scored his last eight successes (including the downing of 48-victory German ace Werner Voss) in SE 5a B525 between 9 September and 11 October 1917. Following Rhys Davids' death in action on 27 October 1917, the aircraft had its individual letter 'I' (which was repeated in white on the uppersurface of the top starboard wing and in black on the undersurface of the port lower wing – see Planform 6) changed to 'V'. It was then issued to fellow ace Capt William Fielding-Johnson MC and Bar DFC of C Flight. In March 1918 B525 was passed on to No 2 Sqn, AFC, and Lt A L Paxton scored a victory with it. When with No 56 Sqn, the aircraft bore the unit's standard broad white fuselage band marking. Its wheel covers, quartered in blue, were unique, however.

19 and 19A

SE 5a B4891 of Capt J T B McCudden, No 56 Sqn, Baizieux, France, February 1918

B4891 was by far the most successful SE 5a in terms of aerial victories to see combat in World War 1, with no fewer than 33 aircraft falling to its guns between 5 December 1917 and 18 March 1918. Some 31 of these victories were claimed by No 56 Sqn's ranking ace, Capt J T B McCudden VC DSO and Bar MC and Bar MM CdG (the last two kills were credited to fellow ace Maj C M Crowe). Originally, McCudden's primary SE 5a had been B4863, marked with a white 'G', although he switched to B4891 – after claiming six victories in B35 – in December 1917. This aircraft, marked with a white '6', was eventually fitted with a red spinner taken from a German LVG that McCudden had downed on 30 November 1917. The spinner reportedly gave the SE 5a a slightly increased top speed. The fighter also boasted raised fuselage sides, possibly to keep out the cold when stalking two-seaters at high altitudes. B4891 was marked with the standard 450 mm white band around its rear fuselage, as well as the number '6' in white and black on its wing surfaces (see scrap view 19A)

20

SE 5a C1096 of Capt H J Burden, No 56 Sqn, Valheureux, France, August 1918

Another high-scoring airframe with No 56 Sqn, C1096 was credited with 13 aircraft destroyed whilst being flown by Canadian Capt 'Hank' Burden DSO DFC between 2 May and 12 August 1918. The fighter features the unit's late war identification markings of two inverted white bars just forward of the tail. The aircraft's individual 'V' was repeated on the upper starboard and lower port wings in white and dark blue, respectively. Note also the SE 5a's blue wheel covers. It is

believed that at some stage in its brief life the aircraft also bore the name *Maybe* in white on the lower part of the engine area, immediately below the blue plaque seen here adorned with a winged St Christopher emblem. Finally, the fighter's propeller had a red boss with white edging.

21

SE 5a D6953 of Capt J W Rayner, No 60 Sqn, Baizieux, France, October 1918

All of No 60 Sqn's SE 5as were marked with two large white bars immediately forward of the tailplane, as seen here on D6953. This aircraft was assigned to A Flight commander Capt John Rayner, hence the white 'A' aft of the fuselage roundel. He claimed all five of his victories with D6953 between 5 September and 25 October 1918, and youthful ace Capt Alexander Beck DFC got a sixth (his tenth overall) on 29 October. Note the fighter's red wheel covers.

22

SE 5a D6945 of Lt A Beck, No 60 Sqn, Boffles, France, August 1918

When still a lieutenant, Alexander Beck claimed his first four (of eleven) victories in D6945 between 8 and 31 August 1918. It too featured thick white fuselage bands just forward of the tailplane, while the individual aircraft letter 'U' was painted below the cockpit and on the upper port wing.

23

SE 5a D278 of Capt E Mannock, No 74 Sqn, Clairmarais North, France, April 1918

'Mick' Mannock used D278 when No 74 Sqn first flew to France at the end of March 1918, and as he was A Flight commander at the time, it carried a white 'A' aft of the fuselage roundel. No 74 Sqn's marking was a white horizontal bar on the top, bottom and sides of the fuselage. Mannock claimed 17 victories with this machine between 12 April and 26 May, making it one of the RAF's highest-scoring SE 5as. D278 was eventually written off when a Camel crashed into it while stationary on the ground on 2 June 1918.

24

SE 5a C1117 of Capt J I T Jones, No 74 Sqn, Clairmarais North, France, June 1918

C1117 was yet another high-scoring No 74 Sqn SE 5a, being used by the unit's ranking ace, 'Taffy' Jones, to claim 15 victories between 17 May and 18 June 1918. Following such sustained combat, the fighter was declared war-weary in late June and struck off charge. Featuring No 74 Sqn's white horizontal bar marking, C1117's aircraft letter was changed to 'T' (for Taffy) just prior to its withdrawal from service.

25

SE 5a D6856 of Capt A F W Beauchamp Proctor, No 84 Sqn, Bertangles, France, August 1918

SE 5a 'ace of aces' 'Proccy' Beauchamp Proctor scored 54 victories in seven different aircraft while serving with No 84 Sqn. The leading airframe in terms of kills was D6856, which the South African used to claim 16 victories between 8 August and 7 September 1918. He was then forced to switch to C1911 when D6856 was written off in an accident on 16 September 1918. The scout bore no personal markings to identify its assignment to No 84 Sqn's leading ace, just the unit's sloping bars on either side of the roundel and blue wheel covers with a white centre, denoting C Flight.

26

SE 5a C1904 of Maj W A Bishop, No 85 Sqn, Petit Synthe, France, June 1918

The SE 5as of No 85 Sqn used a white hexagonal symbol on the fuselage sides aft of the cockade, with individual letters below the cockpit. This letter, again in white, was repeated on the top starboard wing, mid-way between the gun mounting and the roundel. C1904, which appeared on the fin in white, was No 85 Sqn's most successful SE 5a, with Maj Bishop claiming 13 victories with it in just five days between 15 and 19 June 1918 (he was credited with five on the latter date alone). The fighter was then flown by Capt Spencer Horn MC, who scored his final five (of thirteen) victories in C1904 between 7 July and 17 September. Capt W H Longton DFC and two Bars also claimed his fourth kill with it on 24 July.

27

SE 5a D6851 of Lt E W Springs, No 85 Sqn, St-Omer, France, June 1918

Future 16-victory ace Lt Elliott White Springs scored three of his four victories while with No 85 Sqn in this aircraft in June 1918 – he later claimed 12 kills flying Camels with the USAS's 148th Aero Squadron. In the famous No 85 Sqn line up photograph taken at London Colney (see page 77), Springs is seen sat in D6851, which has a white 'X' on its fuselage side but a white 'T' on its top wing! Either the fighter had recently experienced a wing swap, or aircraft 'T' had been changed to 'X' and the photograph was taken prior to the top wing being repainted. Springs crashed in this machine on 27 June after being shot-up by an observer in a German two-seater.

28

SE 5a D372 of Capt J M Robb, No 92 Sqn, Serny, France, August 1918

Future Air Chief Marshal Sir James Robb KBE GCB DSO DFC flew D372 with No 92 Sqn in the summer of 1918, scoring two of his seven victories with it. The fighter was marked with the number '1' behind the fuselage roundel, but ahead of the unit marking of three sloping white bars. This SE 5a was lost on 5 September when fellow ace Lt H B Good was shot down and killed in it fighting with Jasta 37 near Cambrai.

29

SE 5a C9539 of Capt H G Forrest, No 2 Sqn, AFC, Baizieux, France, April 1918

C9539 was the joint high-scoring SE 5a flown by No 2 Sqn, AFC, in 1918, with its pilots claiming 12 victories in total – D6860 was also credited with a similar number of aircraft destroyed. Eleven of the kills were made by Capt Henry Forrest DFC between 22 March and 2 June 1918, whilst Lt (later Captain) R W McKenzie MC scored the fighter's first success (and his second of six victories) on 19 February 1918. The Australian-manned unit's identification marking was, appropriately, a white boomerang, although this was later changed to a single vertical white bar below the cockpit (see Profile 30). C9539's individual letter 'V' was present both on the fuselage and uppersurface of the port top wing.

30

SE 5a E5765 of Capt E E Davies, No 2 Sqn, AFC, Auchel, France, November 1918

E5765 was one of the newest SE 5as issued to No 2 Sqn, AFC, and it was used by Capt Ernest Davies DFC to claim the last four of his seven kills, between 1 October and 4 November. The fighter's individual letter 'A' immediately behind the fuselage cockade was repeated on the uppersurface of the starboard top wing. Note also the revised squadron marking of a single white vertical bar below the cockpit. This aircraft also featured white wheel covers as a flight marking.

31

SE 5a D6995 of Lt F Alberry, No 2 Sqn, AFC, Auchel, France, November 1918

Australia's only one-legged ace, Tasmanian Lt Frank Alberry DCM claimed all seven of his victories in D6995 between 16 September and 4 November 1918. A veteran of the Gallipoli campaign in 1915, Alberry subsequently saw action in France with the Australian infantry until his right kneecap was shattered by a bullet on 27 July 1916. His leg was amputated above the knee as a result, and upon his recovery, Alberry successfully petitioned His Majesty King George V for a transfer to the RFC. D6995 was marked with a large white 'Y' aft of the roundel, which was repeated on the uppersurface of the starboard top wing.

Planform 3

SE 5 A8909 of Capt P B Prothero, No 56 Sqn, Estrée-Blanche, France, July 1917

Early No 56 Sqn ace Capt P B 'Bruce' Prothero claimed five of his victories in this aircraft between 23 May and 11 July 1917. Brought in to the unit as A Flight commander to replace the fallen Capt Albert Ball, Prothero was killed in action on 26 July 1917 when shot down by Artur Muth of Jasta 27. While no squadron marking was allocated at this time, Prothero's fighter was marked with the letters 'AI' on either side of the fuselage roundel and on the fuselage decking, as shown here.

BIBLIOGRAPHY

Fortunately many airmen had their memoirs printed. Books that have been referred to in the text include the following;
Wings over the Somme by G H Lewis
Combat Report by W C Lambert
Survivor's Story by G E Gibbs
Farewell to Wings by C A Lewis
King of Air Fighters by J I T Jones
Flying Fury by J T B McCudden
Mac's Memoirs by G H Cunningham
A Yankee Ace in the RAF by J H Morrow and Earl Rogers

The following reference books also proved to be most useful;
The SE 5 File by Ray Sturtivant and Gordon Page
British Aviation Squadron Markings of World War 1 by Les Rogers
SE 5/SE 5a Squadrons by Les Rogers
The Aeroplanes of the RFC Military Wing by J M Bruce
High in the Empty Blue by Alex Reve

INDEX

References to illustrations are shown in **bold**. Plates are shown
with page and caption locators in brackets, the prefix 'Plan'
denoting 'Planform'.